Instinct for Survival

INSTINCT FOR
Survival

ESSAYS BY PAT C. HOY II

THE UNIVERSITY OF GEORGIA PRESS   ATHENS & LONDON

Paperback edition published in 2012
by the University of Georgia Press
Athens, Georgia 30602
www.ugapress.org
© 1992 by Pat C. Hoy II
All rights reserved
Designed by Sandra Strother Hudson
Set in Sabon by Tseng Information Systems, Inc.

Printed digitally in the United States of America

The Library of Congress has cataloged the hardcover
edition of this book as follows:
Hoy, Pat C.
Instinct for survival : essays / by Pat C. Hoy II.
152 p. : ill. ; 24 cm.
ISBN 0-8203-1394-7
1. Hoy, Pat C. 2. United States. Army—Biography.
3. Soldiers—United States—Biography. 4. Educators—
United States—Biography. I. Title.
CT275.H6593 A3   1992
973.9'092—dc20   91-17720
[B]

Paperback ISBN-13: 978-0-8203-3937-5
ISBN-10: 0-8203-3937-7

British Library Cataloging-in-Publication Data available

Some of the essays in this volume first appeared in *Agni*:
"The Spirit Was Willing and So Was the Flesh";
Sewanee Review: "Mosaics of Southern Masculinity:
Small-Scale Mythologies," "Soldiering"; and *Virginia
Quarterly Review*: "Imagining Lives of Our Own."

"Goings and Comings" is reprinted from *Home Ground:
Southern Autobiography*, by J. Bill Berry, by permission of
the University of Missouri Press. Copyright 1991 by the
Curators of the University of Missouri.

For My Parents

NAN JO HOY
PATRICK CLEBURN HOY

Contents

Soldiering
1

Goings and Comings
23

Mosaics of Southern Masculinity
43

Imagining Lives of Our Own
66

Conversing with Images
85

The Spirit Was Willing and
So Was the Flesh
103

Mortality
125

Immortality
140

SURVIVAL is on my mind these days. The urge to hang on seems deeply embedded in my soul. Perhaps it's no more than my natural resistance to death. I just don't know, but I do know that when I manage to get close to that spirit of endurance, the events I'm writing about seem to *reverberate* into eternity. They speak to me of perseverance.

THIS COLLECTION OF ESSAYS grounds itself in lives that have been lived close to the earth. I dedicate it to my parents, two people who loved each other desperately for ten years and then parted. My father went his own way; my mother dug her feet in and lasted. She didn't know how to give in. Both of them taught me the lessons of life—one *in absentia,* one ever-present. From them, I got my bearings. From them I learned to stand on my own. They continue, long past their deaths, to nourish my life.

Instinct for Survival

Soldiering

Only the dead have seen the end of war.
PLATO

ON JANUARY 1, 1945, my brother Dub and his B-26 were, I suppose, blown to bits in a flak-infested sky over Germany. We never really knew the whole story. The euphemisms of war prolonged the agony and encouraged hope. An empty grave still waits in the Luxembourg cemetery. No remains—the War Department would say passively from the outset—were found, ever.

Sometime during that first week of January, I was called out of my first-grade room and given the news. I don't remember how they told me, but I do remember being outside in the school yard with my back against the side of the lunchroom, my mom's arms around me. Ellisene, my older sister, was standing there with her, I think. Their words are lost to me. What linger in my memory are the days, and then the weeks, and then the months of waiting. I watched the women cluster together, time after time, grieving: my mom, my sister, Dub's fiancée. There were no men around. My other brother was in Cairo. My dad was on a ship, in San Diego, somewhere, gone.

I recall when the European part of that war ended, recall the parade down Main Street, the band playing as it marched by, the music and the hoopla—the celebration. I remember, as if it were just yesterday, how I squatted down inside that smelly stack of tires out in front of my dad's stores, me inside the tires that were stacked up along side the street, me down in there in the darkness, wondering, me down inside dirtying my hands, being by myself, hunkered, playing, apart from the show moving along the road.

I was young, too young, I now think, to experience Dub's loss in a very personal way. I still can't remember any of the things they kept wanting me to remember—how much he loved me and hated to leave me when he went off to training camp, things like that. He had already been away from home almost two years, and I was only six on that New Year's Day when he died. But I held on anyway, all through my childhood, to the German bayonet he had sent home for me. It was there in a trunk in the attic almost forty years later when I went back for Mom's funeral. His trunk was full of other remains . . . his pictures, the bayonet, the Air Medal, his dopp kit, his double-edge razor, his letters from home, one or two khaki uniforms, the Army Air Corp patches still intact on the starched and folded shirts, the paper bands still around them.

The parade, that parade down Main Street didn't bring Dub back, and it didn't stop the women's suffering. It didn't bring my dad, who survived, back to me and Mom either. But neither did the war rip that little community asunder; that was the miracle of it all. Hamburg, Arkansas, was there when the war started, and it was there when it ended. Altered, yes. Preserved, yes. Destroyed, hardly. Death was not the end of it. Some folks died, others left, but Hamburg still stands.

At that very young age, I became, against all desire, an observer of the aftermath of war. A quarter of a century later, when I went off to another war, I went to honor a commitment. I was not responding to the sound of the guns. Going was a matter of obligation. I owed some service to the state. When I left, I left pretty sure I'd make it back. I left with preservation on my mind.

MARY LEE SETTLE claims that war gives men a chance to find out the answer to the most "atavistic question" in their souls, a chance to find out whether they will fight or turn tail. I think most of us answer that question in more private ways, on other fields. Ron Kovich, born on the Fourth of July, didn't, and he ended up a paraplegic for life, part of the price he paid for a misplaced dream about heroism.

I answered the atavistic question for myself one afternoon in the tenth grade when I tackled Albert Kusterin. He was a junior, the best running back on the team. Albert looked mean, almost possessed. He ran like a deer and seemed protected. Those of us coming up from junior high knew he was fragile enough to be explosive. I tackled him anyway. Hitting him felt good. On the next play, I hit him again, nailed him as hard as I could to see if it would hurt me. He glared disapproval as I returned to my linebacker position feeling strangely exhilarated. But there was more to it. On that practice field in the sweltering heat of an August afternoon when I was but sixteen, I pulled back inside, troubled. Cracking Albert Kusterin's ass felt too good. Whatever I needed to know about turning tail, I found out that day. I didn't need war to give me the answers. What I found out on that hot August afternoon in south Arkansas I never forgot. Getting high on someone else's pain is serious business.

I went to war primarily because I had decided at seventeen or eighteen to go to West Point. At that impressionable age, going to West Point had less to do with war than with a way for a boy to leave home. The catalog promised that I would learn to be as comfortable in a foxhole as I would be dining with the queen of England. I liked the queen of England part. The lasting consequences of my decision didn't really hit me until I was thirty. Glamor and hard work and promotion and opportunity had kept me from facing the fact of war until I had to go.

As an artillery officer, I had for years prepared units for combat, had trained hundreds of men, knew my own business inside out, could put steel on the target with the best of them. But I hadn't actually faced what it meant for *me* to go to war until a very good friend called from Washington while I was in graduate school at the University of Pennsylvania, announced a change of policy about West Point teaching assignments, and told me to start packing my bags. We laughed. Later, my wife and I cried. Tim was not yet three. Patrick, our older son, had been born in Arkansas five years earlier while I was in Korea—on what the Army called a *short* tour. We had already moved five times in the last five years.

It was not until nearly twenty years later, just a couple of years ago, that I began to consider what actually got me to West Point and then to war. At first I held my mom accountable. I thought for a long time that she had sent me to redeem herself, to make up for other losses, but now I measure that notion against the risk she certainly knew she was taking. She sent me off to become a soldier, knowing full well what that meant.

So now I have to own up to the fact that there was something I liked about the idea of soldiering, something I couldn't put my finger on for a long, long time. There were my two brothers, especially Willard who came back from the war, finished a career in the Air Force as a Senior Master Sergeant, raised four boys, and still died young, near the end of a second career close to home in Arkansas. Dub's death and Willard's service in North Africa no doubt impressed me, but not nearly so much as the life I lived without them, the life that left me during my formative years without any men to point the way.

One of my favorite photographs shows me sitting on the front porch steps of a house on Main Street in Hamburg where my sister-in-law lived during part of the war. I'm holding an 8 × 10 photograph of Willard in his Army Air Corps uniform, showing the picture to Scott, Willard's oldest son. I'm eight; Scott's three. The three of us are there, in the picture, together. Now, after all those years, I see what's not in the picture. Someone put us there on those steps with Willard. Scott and I surely didn't think of posing that way. Dell believed that Willard, her husband, rebuilding aircraft engines in Cairo, Egypt, needed to know something about what was going on at home, what was going on there on Main Street in Hamburg while he was off counting days in a land too far away for anyone in south Arkansas to imagine. But there was something even more important to Dell. Willard was off in that place because he believed our very lives might depend on his being there; she did too. Willard had something to do with our survival.

WHEN I WENT AWAY to West Point, I took with me a notion of my own about survival, but I didn't understand it until twenty years later sitting on a saddle horse, making my way up a creek bed in Wyoming. I had gone there with two other writers, one of them my friend. I was anxious to see what professionals do on assignment, and I wanted to see how I would stack up against them. I guess I wanted to know if I could hold my own as a writer. But I came back from Wyoming, twenty-seven years into an Army career, convinced, finally, that I was a soldier. Some part of me always would be, always had been. I knew why, at long last.

We had gotten to the first camping spot the evening before, at the end of a long, disorienting day. Gretel Ehrlich, my writer friend, had driven the four of us in a pickup to a spot between Jackson Hole and Dubois. The horses were waiting. So were Press Stevens and his helpers. Others were waiting too, so we ate our sack lunches in a hurry, watched someone else load our gear, mounted the horses, listened to words of wisdom—"Ride your stirrups long" . . . "Give Minny the reins, trust her"—and began our trek to the campsite, crossing what we thought was the most rugged terrain we would ever see: straight up, straight down, nine of us strung out in a line with nine other pack horses, up and down for three hours on dusty little trails more narrow at the bottom than our horses' bodies a few hands higher up.

I remember little about that first evening, only the rushing, shallow streams that surrounded our campsite, the red disk of the sun's reflection I drank from the icy water... my sore body. I helped unload the horses, but paid no attention. Press, our guide, Gretel's husband, asked the men in the group to put up tents. We did. Sleep came just after the Milky Way appeared. We were beyond the smoke.

By the time we woke up, the wrangler was coming back with the horses. Press had his collapsible stove blazing and was ready to pour the pancakes on an old cast iron griddle he kept rotating with a pair of channel lock pliers. "Got a cold spot on the stove," he said.

Press hadn't done much talking the day before. I had watched him set things in motion, but hadn't gotten to hear much of what he said. I could see that he said very little. When he spoke, men moved. He looked like a cowboy on his horse, more at home there in the saddle than he would have ever been back in Atlanta, I suspected. His accent was too flat to be southern. And he didn't look like an art history major, but I knew from Gretel's essays that he was.

I began to like him when he put me to work after breakfast. He started talking about packhorses and Custer and Indians and thousands of soldiers with hundreds of horses. We were a miniature army; that was his point. We had loading to do, and he had a loading plan. We still called them loading plans in the army I was in.

Press's plan called for nine loads, split into eighteen stacks. Each pair of stacks would be balanced for the horses' comfort (he had scales to use when he didn't trust his own feel), placed on the ground and split far enough apart for the horses to pass through. Press put the plan in motion. We were expected to be alert, join in where we thought we could help. I was on the opposite side of a horse from Press before anyone had issued a word of instructions, holding up a load of three bed rolls, three bags of tent poles, and filler. I don't know how I got there.

"Pat," he said, "I'm gonna tie 'em high and tight. You take the rope from under the belly, bring it under the corner of the load like this and pass it back over the top to me." Press had gotten around to my side somehow. "Keep it tight. I'll take up the slack, you lift up the load and keep the canvas cover straight." He disappeared back to the other side of the horse. I couldn't see over the load.

"I don't hire many short packers," I heard him say from the other side as we began the back and forth motion that finally turned into a rhythm as we moved down the line of horses. He talked, half to himself, half to me during the hour or so we spent across horses from one another.

During that week, I watched him move us around, giving us as much work as he knew we could stand, keeping each of us involved somehow in the survival of the whole lot. Watching Press I began to think about leadership again and remembered that someone years ago had told me in a class at West Point that good leaders know how to get soldiers to work willingly and cheerfully in the interest of survival. I thought again about heroism and began to see quite clearly that heroism and soldiering have more to do with preservation and survival than with destruction and death. But that was not the story we had been telling ourselves through the sixties. The story of our survival had become a story about dominoes, a string of dominoes that led to Communist territories far away, so far away few of us at home could believe what would happen when and if the dominoes fell, few except the men who made up the tale.

And when that tale seemed too far-fetched, the men in Washington made up another one. Bomb them long enough and often enough and they'll see the light . . . arc-light it was called. Exterminate the brutes, Brando had said in that movie about darkness and power and obliteration. Brando's story, Kurtz's story, Conrad's story had become the story of the sixties, the story part of the nation told itself in order to live. We would save ourselves by destruction. That was the story we had begun to tell, and it seemed to me very different from the one Dell told herself while she waited for Willard to come back from Cairo. As I listened to that new story during those years of turmoil and considered how my life was being spent, I began to wonder what we were preserving.

Almost from the beginning of that pack trip in Wyoming, I found myself falling into Press's rhythms, and I began to see that my soldiering set me apart from the others on the trip, all of the others except Press. For the first time in over thirty years, I could watch someone else pull a group together. I had no leadership responsibilities. But I knew long before the others what had to be done, knew that we couldn't make it for nine days on Press's energy. He was riding, after all, on a plastic donut, having crawled out of the wilderness only three weeks before, flagged down a ride in a pickup, made his way to a hospital, survived the operation, and returned to do his duty. He was an outfitter. Never mind the donut; never mind the tent we set up for his sitz baths. Complaining was not his business. He had nine people, eighteen horses, and provisions to look after. Press came last, after everything else was taken care of, after he had gotten us to do willingly (and sometimes cheerfully) what we needed to do to last.

The second day out, riding up Cub Creek heading for the high ground, I was in a poetic mood, trying to see as much as I could. Ted Hoagland was suffering from cataract problems, so we were all trying to see for him too, staying alert, looking for the elk or the hawks or the patches of color that no one would want to miss anyway. It was a lazy, peaceful day, the sun bright on the yellow and green scrubby growth along the creekbeds. We were actually riding through an immensely long valley, mountains rising up so high I had to lean back in my saddle to see their peaks. On my left, I seemed almost to be rubbing up against their base; they were upon me, bearing down close so that as I looked up, I could work my way up the crevices, grabbing hold here and there, climbing my way up. When I got near an avalanche course, high up, I saw in my mind's eye those three Chinamen from Yeats's poem, "Lapis Lazuli." Up there near the top of one of those mountains, I saw "Their ancient, glittering eyes" looking down on what they would consider the whole "tragic scene." "Gaiety," Yeats wrote, "transfiguring all that dread."

As I looked back down, across the scene, I was surprised at myself, surprised that as I looked across the wide valley, I saw the terrain curve into the base of the mountains, saw right there a place fit for an artillery battery, spread out in a lazy W, the guns pointing back down the valley from where we had come, protecting everything that lay behind them to the east, everything from Wyoming to Oklahoma, or Arkansas, or Virginia. I thought for just a moment of the Indians facing east into those guns, and I wondered why we would have been so interested in taking the land from the only people who actually knew how to live on it. Why, I wondered, as I rode along amidst all that primeval beauty, was I putting artillery in place, why at that moment were Yeats and the earth and the Indians and three Chinamen dancing around inside my head. And then I knew, knew as sure as I knew my name, that Yeats had been wrong. Old civilizations need not come and go; the scene need not be tragic. We make it so. Telling and retelling our old, familiar stories of derring-do, acting them out, we perpetuate the tragic scene. And there I was, a soldier to the core, torn between my love of the land, the sheer beauty of it, and my need to put my guns in place, to defend it. There I was, for the first time in my life, in a position to tell my own version of the story.

Sitting here now, trying to fit together a mosaic of my own

masculinity, my mind is drawn inexorably to a parade at West Point where I sit with a woman from across the river in Garrison, New York. I am a teacher of literature, forty-nine years old, serving my twelfth year on the faculty of the Military Academy. She had lived there in Garrison, just across the Bear Mountain bridge, all her life and had never once been to a full-dress parade. I suspect that over her life's span, the *New York Times* had persuaded her she ought to be a bit wary of the goings-on in that granite fortress. I remember sending her into tears one evening at a dinner party when I suggested there might actually be evidence, verifiable evidence, that Russia was indeed helping build a highway of sorts from those other Americas right up through Mexico. What bothered her most about my suggestion was that the *Times* piece she'd read the previous Sunday had made it perfectly clear there was no threat from our south, and she was very upset that I thought there might be other news fit to print.

Sitting there with Nancy at the beginning of the ceremony, I was keenly aware of our differences, aware that I had never seen a West Point parade with a person so skittish about ceremony. But when I sensed that even she was keeping time with the music, I relaxed and found myself looking at the patterns of the trees' shadows playing on the granite walls across the parade field. I saw in those patterns that day, evanescent as they were, a kind of permanence etching itself into the granite. I saw something in the design of things that would last. I had never seen it before. West Point had been there before my time, and it would survive me. It would outlast me and my kind. I knew too that if it didn't last, the country would be in trouble, serious trouble, because something in its very foundation would be missing, something that had to do with stability and preservation. Something that had been empowered by Congress to make things last.

Out there in Wyoming, I didn't think much about West Point; the land itself was stirring my soul, and I began to try to figure out why I had things primal on my mind, why I could at long last start to see how certain events in my life conspired to make me a soldier. Some of them, like those parades, seemed so farfetched, yet they began to come together, making a statement, telling me what I hadn't ever wanted to know before.

Riding out of that wilderness after eight days, I was already looking back on the experience of nine people finding a way to live together despite their differences, nine people trying to work out patterns for themselves that would give them a stake in the group yet keep them separate, whole. Such a thing can happen with strong-willed people, and it did on that trip. The work was communal, the conversations almost always private. Riding out of the valley, in the snow and the rain, I had six hours to think, and I came to realize that my most intense memories were deeply mythic. Timeless. If Press had gone back to the cavalry and packhorses, seeing us as a miniature army, I had gone back to a later time . . . or was it earlier, to flying horses, helicopters, thirty-six loads slung beneath their bellies, six of those loads always 105mm howitzers. Those were unit moves involving more than 125 men, tons of equipment, moves that went from sunup to sundown, day after day, week after week, for a year in Vietnam. Moves planned for survival.

There in Wyoming, we rode the horses; they carried the loads; they carried us and we watched them, lived with them, came to know how much we had to depend on them and on each other. Wyoming would have been a perfect training ground for young lieutenants, much more demanding than the Army's National Training Center in the desert where everything is on call, high tech and fast, everything, that is, except the human element. In Wyoming, the lieutenants would have had to worry about preservation as well as destruction. Press loaded for the horses' comfort. He liked tight, clean, balanced loads. No flapping canvas. No slack. Watching him, I rediscovered spirituality behind that kind of perfection, saw for the first time in years how simple the principle: work, good, hard, competent work yields satisfaction, not so much self-satisfaction as the satisfaction of a community in the throes of survival.

That kind of work, for a man, is its own reward. I was surprised on that trip that with four good-looking women, my male imagination turned to teamwork and friendly games: putting up tents well, doing tasks well without wasting energy. Out there, close to the earth, I found more and more pleasure in the work itself. Around the campfire, at the end of a long day, I wanted to cook, wanted a more satisfying stake in Press's work. I really wanted to be competent enough to lead the whole pack train, but I had to face the fact that I didn't know enough about the wilderness to live in it on my own. Had I been as good as Press, I too could have had a hold on the secrets of survival and could have had the ultimate pleasure of leading others to turn hard work into something lasting, something permanent.

In Vietnam nothing was permanent; nothing lasted. The war was a shock from beginning to end, the most boring experience of my entire life. It sits there in my memory, a red badge of capitulation. I can't get rid of it, and I can't wear it with honor. Going to Vietnam is the most deeply ambivalent thing I ever did. I was against the war politically, yet I was a soldier bound by my duty. I had to go, but it's the only thing I've ever done that I wouldn't do again . . . and yet I'm glad I did it. The sad part is that no one can take it away from me, and no one wants to. No one can help me with its burden. That's the supreme price soldiers pay. I went to Vietman, as I've already said, because I owed some service to the state that had raised me from boyhood. But being professional to the core did not relieve me of doubts.

During the entire plane ride to Vietnam, I tried to imagine what it would be like, what of the war might coincide with what I had read and studied. My shock on arrival had a great deal to do with my imagined realities of war. I had expected to land in a combat zone. Instead, I found myself in a military city and couldn't believe my eyes. I was angry and felt cheated. It seemed a worse hoax than I had imagined it might be.

For a year, I was the operations officer for a 105mm howitzer battalion. I moved four artillery batteries by helicopter at the whim of any of three division commanders in and around the III Corps tactical zone. A commander called for fire power; we moved. My routine work, apart from motivating the men, was to select new positions, develop movement plans, and supervise the moves from fire base to fire base, those small, circular suicidal positions where the men had to live in the middle of nowhere. On the perimeter of each fire base was an infantry battalion minus a lot of people and equipment. In the middle of the circle were six howitzers and the artillerymen who sat for days on end waiting for the Viet Cong, or for an order from me to move again, lock, stock, and barrel. It was a circular war. No front lines. No safe zones. These fire bases were established to draw out the VC, to lure them to attack. When they worked, it was a red-hot affair, on the one hand something like New York harbor under the direction of Lee Iacocca on the Fourth of July, on the other something bloody awful.

Almost every day, I went out to those isolated fire bases. Hermes I was—in one world at night, in another during the day. I was the emissary from the base camp, the man from the land of the post exchange. In the field, I was a reminder to those men that there was a way out. I was also a reminder of tough, demanding standards. My real job (the one I gave myself) was to keep American soldiers alive. Survival. That was the name of my game in that other wilderness. Few of my men died. Two of those who did died out of boredom . . . or a desire to find out whether they would turn tail and run. They volunteered for something extra and lost their lives.

Those soldiers on the fire bases formed one of two communities in Vietnam, a community of men sitting in the middle of nowhere, waiting, waiting for the VC or waiting for the movement order. The other community was not much to my liking. It was the one I lived in—a community resting on the shaky foundation of assumed privilege. I stayed out of it as much as I could, but it affected the way I did my business every night. I had to reckon with it. At the headquarters across the airfield from our battalion area, the group commander had a chapel; inside the chapel, he had a handball court. He also had an officer's mess in another building, and every night he held court: sit-down dinner, wine, china, movie, popcorn, the works. Long about 2330 every night, he would amble back over to his office desk for a little snooze. Sometime about midnight, I'd be told who would move the next morning, how many helicopters we'd be allocated, who the reinforced unit would be. Then, and not until then, I could go to work by radio to get the word out to the troops on the ground who had to be ready to greet the first helicopters at dawn, loads slung, balanced, weighed to rest easy under the belly of the chopper.

Out there in the field one night, in one of those circular outposts, a young captain named Lesniac earned his second Silver Star. He directed his firing battery against a VC attack for over four hours. This was close-in, hair-raising stuff. They fired almost 1,500 rounds directly at the enemy. The attack was so intense and so concentrated, the infantrymen finally shot red flares in the air to signal that they were going below ground into the perimeter bunkers. On that signal the artillerymen began firing special flechette ammunition. That beehive round would go off just after it cleared the howitzer tube, sending out a cone-shaped sector of death, thousands of tiny arrows the likes of which would stop every one of those other archers at Agincourt dead in their tracks. That night Al Lesniac and his men shot over twenty beehives right at the perimeter when the Viet Cong got close enough to start laying their tiny bamboo ladders on the wire to make it easier to get across.

I arrived at the fire-support base just after first light and could see from the air that the VC had already carried off most of their dead before daybreak, but the weapons were everywhere, scattered all over the earth. Our men were out with the Jeeps and trailors loading up the AK-47's, the RPG's, the detritus of war. On the ground, face to face with the men, I found them surprisingly calm, intact. They had survived, all of them, and they had done it through teamwork and instinct and trust. Lesniac was smiling when he walked up to me, reminding me that as I had left the afternoon before, he had invited me to spend the night. He looked a little disheveled, but not at all like a man who had been put to the test. Already, he was starting to get his uniform together as he walked around pointing out what had to be done to get ready for another day.

It wasn't long before the group artillery commander made his way down from the skies, only twenty-five or thirty minutes past his morning coffee from the white china cup, and when he arrived, Lesniac, always the good soldier, rushed over to the helicopter pad to meet him, looking almost as put together as the commander himself, starched and erect as an Army football player greeting the president in Washington in the aftermath of a victory over Navy. Everything about Lesniac was in order except his right trouser leg; he hadn't managed to tuck that in his boot yet.

"Morning, sir. Captain Lesniac, reporting to the Group Commander."

"Captain, get your trouser leg bloused," he said.

"Yes, sir. Sir, what would you like to see this morning?" The senior commanders took little interest in what had actually happened the night before, past the counting of bodies and weapons. Somehow they must have figured they were responsible for Lesniac's success and saw no need to give him much credit there on the ground he had defended. It wasn't sacred territory, of course, but there in Vietnam it was all those men had to hang on to, and together they had done it, preserving whatever there was to preserve of their own dignity. They were a long way from home.

I returned home in the grip of a paradox. I had left for Vietnam knowing we had no business there. I didn't buy into the domino game. But there in country, on the ground, exigencies overshadowed politics. Everything I did seemed justified in light of my being there. To get through it, I did what West Point had taught me to do. I tucked my soul away and got on with the job, displacing myself in the routine of work, surrendering to task. I expect every man or woman who goes to war has to do that to some extent as a means of survival. I had learned a little bit about surviving as a kid back in Hamburg, learned by watching the women, learned not to tuck soul away in times of distress. But if those women had given me an imagination honed on suffering, West Point had done its best to teach me to rein in that imagination, to put it on hold. To get through West Point and Korea and Vietnam, I had to tuck soul away.

Tucking it away, I paid a price. When I walked onto that plane one day in Saigon, walked into Travis Air Force Base in San Francisco the next, and walked later that day into the airport at Little Rock, I was a displaced person and didn't know it. I had returned from a bizarre world to a world even more bizarre. A couple of weeks later, we were at West Point. In less than a month, I was teaching freshman composition to future Army officers. Vietnam was a thing of the past (I thought); no one talked about it; no one wanted to talk about it. We buried it, all of us.

Even at West Point, there was no community to come back to. Men might tell war stories, but they didn't talk about their feelings with one another. They didn't talk about the war itself, what it had been like to them, how they actually felt about the politics of it all. For some reason hard to fathom, even the humanists in the English department didn't talk about the deleterious effects of a war that left its soldiers suspended between the world of combat and the world of societal disorder, left them without a community to come home to, left them at odds with themselves. Even West Point was shaken by the war, unsure—perhaps for the first time in its history—about Duty and Honor. Nothing was quite as it should have been.

Only now can I see how Vietnam shaped much of my later life. I had not realized until just two years ago about the tucking away of soul and what that had cost me. Gretel Ehrlich, writing her own book about war, asked me what Vietnam was like. Hers was the first question anyone, and I mean anyone, had ever asked me about that experience. I had been back eighteen years. Answering her, I began to see what had happened, how my recovery had not begun until five years after I had come back, when in the midst of a marital crisis, I had to stop to figure out who the hell I was and what was important to me. In the middle of that crisis, my head started to clear a little from my psychological investigations, and during a recess in a general court martial—one in which I was a board member—I walked over to a typewriter, wrote the chairman of the English department at West Point, and told him I wanted to return to teaching.

Altogether, I spent fourteen years of a twenty-eight year Army career teaching future officers. Seven months ago, I turned in my spurs. At my retirement ceremony in Grant Hall, under the portraits of the five-star generals, I spoke to my friends about the nomadic life of an Army family. I had chosen my words thinking about another, more solemn ceremony I had witnessed just weeks before when a tenured faculty member stood for his retirement with his wife, two daughters, and three sons—the sons in Army greens, all graduates of West Point. The retiring professor told us that one of his daughters would also have made a fine cadet had she chosen to be one. He was, of course, retelling the old, old story about the fathers and their progeny.

At my retirement, I wanted to tell that story a different way, and I did, standing with balloons flying over my head, my wife, Ann, and our two sons to my left, and my friend Peter Stromberg, instead of a general, bidding me farewell. Peter chose to recite a poem about a juggler rather than the official narrative of my twenty-eight years of service. I chose to tell within my longer story a story about my sons, a story about how different they were from each other and from me. It began something like this: Once upon a time in Bryn Mawr, Pennsylvania, the children of Pat and Ann Hoy began to transform their parents' lives. That was the story. It was just that simple. I was in graduate school for the last time. We were out of the sheltered Army community, and instead of having to make our own way with a new circle of friends, in a new community, Patrick and Tim did it for us. They formed the bonds.

When it came time for us to leave Bryn Mawr for my tenured post at West Point, Patrick came into my study one night with tears in his eyes. He said, "Dad, I don't want to move." I had no words of consolation. Even though I was going back to the only job I had ever really wanted, I knew I was exacting a heavy price from my children. West Point was not the "envy of their dreams." Nevertheless, after we got back there, and over the years, each in his turn considered a soldier's life, and after thinking it over, knew that he was not cut out for it. They had watched from the wings, and their imaginations had been active, so active, I suspect, they knew too much about the consequences. Soldiering just didn't suit them.

I told our friends assembled in Grant Hall that afternoon at my retirement that if I could take Patrick's wand out of his old leather satchel of magic tricks, and if I could wave that wand over those two young men to create them any way I wanted, I would make them just the way they are. They are creating their own stories as they get on with their lives, and some day, if the rest of us find a way to preserve the world we're all inhabiting, my sons will tell their stories, different as they are from mine.

Just two years before I retired, nine years after Bryn Mawr, eighteen after Vietnam, I finally made a trip to Washington, D.C. I began at long last to unbury a part of my soul that I had tucked away so long ago. There at the Vietnam Memorial, I found Robert Kowalski and Paul Savanauch, those two young soldiers from my unit in Vietnam. They were on the polished walls . . . and so was I. Reflected and reflecting, I had a peaceful but disturbing feeling, seeing myself against the national backdrop, the black lines of the walls extending out beyond themselves to the other monuments, the people there with me in the mirror, climbing on one another's shoulders to place a small piece of paper over the names, climbing on one another's shoulders to play the game we played as children, making a rubbing, creating with pencil and paper a name, an image they could take home, laugh and cry over, hold, save, cherish. We were all there—together—recovering soul, taking it out of its unrightful place, setting free our imaginations, some of us perhaps for the first time.

As I walked along inside the memorial, I thought of one of the cadets Ann and I sponsored at West Point, an Army brat whose military roots run through at least three generations on both sides. I thought of him because I want him to come with me to the memorial someday to read its message. I want to say to him, "These are the names of soldiers who died. You and I—the nation—all of us are responsible. We always are. We are all in this monument together, inescapably here. That is the message."

West Point was never Camelot for me; that's why I was ready to leave it. The Army was never my obsession, never my life. But, of course, West Point and the Army gave me life. It was there that my imagination finally took flight; it was there that we raised our sons. West Point is a magical place, but its magic has little to do with rules and systems and codes. It has to do with deeper values, with preservation, stability, endurance. West Point draws people to it as if it were an ancient philosopher's stone, and it drew me straight out of Hamburg, Arkansas, before I had even an inkling of what it was all about.

MY MIND, back in Hamburg now, abuzz with characters, settles on a community of odd ducks. Conger Knight, mute, hunched, and apelike was as much at home there as Walter Carruth, who showed up a couple of times a week at the back door of the drugstore where I worked, always looking for fifty-cents worth of paregoric. Conway Harris, the druggist, also the self-appointed veterinarian, had run over my brother Dub's bird dog after the war, killing the last of Dub's possessions that nobody else had a claim on. Conway was drunk they said, on a rainy night, and when Jeep died both the women and the men in town had broken hearts. As fate would have it, I ended up working for Conway Harris until he sold out to Bob Drake who was known for the Catholic woman he married, the only one in town. In that drugstore where I worked all through high school, I came to know the town's characters pretty well, came to see finally something of what held the place together.

Jess Etheridge was my favorite character because my relationship with him was so complicated. His brother Hogan was my best friend's grandfather. Hogan's wife, Agnes, was my high school English teacher. His daughter, my good friend's mother, was the first woman I ever saw naked, saw her quite inadvertently through the crack in her bathroom door, standing there straight up in the bathtub, drying herself. I never forgot. Strange lines of complications bound us together in that little hamlet.

Jess was my man about town. He put fear in the hearts of

most young folks who knew him. He said little, stared a lot, and commanded attention wherever he went. When he came into the drugstore where I worked, all of the other clerks left for parts unknown as Mr. Jess took the seat with a view. He wanted to watch the other customers come and go, and I know now that he wanted to be watched too. I approached Jess with caution as he sat there like a middle-aged Lytton Strachey with his long legs intertwined, his cane hooked over the top leg or leaned against the marble-top ice cream table. When he finally took his hat off, his glistening head was smooth as an auk's egg, and the round glasses on his very long face gave him a look I would later think of as intellectual. At the time, I thought little and went about my business with respect.

Always at the outset, Jess cleared his throat deliberately, drawing out a low, long rumble, projecting strange noises all over the store. He ended this performance each time with a droaning hum just before he reached in his coat pocket to pull out a fresh, warm pullet's egg to hand over to me. As he did so, he glanced directly into my eyes for a split second—that was the way he ordered his vanilla milkshake. I knew what he wanted, had to or I would have been dismissed for being too dim-witted to keep up. The fresh egg was for the shake as was the ground nutmeg he brought forth simultaneously from the other pocket and slapped down on the table, staring all the time toward the front of the store, watching to see if anyone was watching him.

I don't know what Jess did with all his waking hours; he didn't work, I know that much. When I saw him outside the store, he was either sitting on the benches over by the post office or walking around the square dressed in neatly pressed khaki trousers and a wool sportcoat, assisted in these constitutionals by that walking cane the "gov'ment" had given him for services rendered in the Great War. My sister tells me he was shell-shocked. Whether he was or not doesn't matter much to this story. What does matter is that Jess had a place to come home to, and he fit in. Had he wanted to talk, he could have. There was a community that understood enough to leave him alone and to include him in it. And so he and Walter and Conger, odd as they were, and John S. White who came back from a later war an ace and an alcoholic, and B. A. Courson who survived the Bataan Death March and ended up the sheriff, came home again to a town that had a place for them. And that, I think, is what just wars are all about. They make things last. They ensure that men and women always have a place to come home to.

Goings and Comings

She is our history, and it is from her simple lap that we fell.
JAMES HILLMAN

I AM BACK AGAIN. There by her side in the nursing home, I have to rouse her into consciousness, but she smiles instantly and pushes her frail body up toward me from the bed. She knows that I have come from New York, at last, and she knows without a doubt that I will not come again. Her ninety-year-old mind, despite the minor strokes, remains alert.

Sinking back on the bed, she stretches out her arms, holding on while pushing me back a bit, getting distance, letting her eyes focus. She wants to see me, wants to look me over, size me up. She's done it all my life. It's always the first thing she does, her way of assessing changes, her way of determining whether I still belong to her. I help her with her glasses, and as I push the frames back across her temples, she reaches up through the space between my arms and takes my face in her hands as she used to do when I was a little boy, holding me gently for a minute, then bringing her fingers down my cheeks, feeling as she does the shape of my face, confirming me by touch as her palms and then her fingers come together below my chin, the tips still touching the underside of my face, moving slightly from side to side, steadying both of us. Only her twitching lower lip betrays her steadfastness. Her eyes, she would say, are steady as the Rock of Gibraltar. But her voice won't work. I hear only deep, raspy guttural sounds. She tries again to extend the greeting beyond touch.

"Hi, honey, I'm glad you're home."

"Yeah, me too, mom. You need to take it easy, okay?"

"I'm gonna be just fine now. Prop me up a bit, you hear."

I do, and she settles into the pillows, dozing a couple of minutes before looking up at me again. I see that our two days will not be time enough.

The phone conversations have been short and labored. I have not seen her this way. My sister, who had lived next door to Mom for years, has been her keeper, first at home before it got too bad and then in the nursing home. I know from Ellisene that Mom is often out of joint with time, traveling back twenty years, sometimes forty or fifty, reliving an old scene. Happy. I had had only one glimpse into those travels. One night when I called Mom told me she was at a party where they were dancing on the tables. I suspected medication was causing her to fantasize. Still I encouraged her to talk about the party, and she moved quickly to another topic, losing interest in me and the conversation.

She had been in the hospital in Crossett then, and to make things worse, the nurses had lost her teeth. Ellisene finally had to drive over from Hamburg and retrace their steps, only to find the teeth wrapped in dirty sheets in the laundry bin. Childlike, hurt, Mom had been beside herself, embarrassed and distraught, publicly disfigured. She had been a strong, independent woman for most of her years. And now her need for help and her excursions into memory characterized her life. She didn't look like Miss Winnie Jones next door had looked two years earlier when Mom walked me around to her room. My good friend's grandmother was shriveled, tucked forever into bed yet very much alive. I thought at the time Mom had taken me over to say hello. Standing now at Mom's bedside, waiting for her to regain consciousness, I wonder whether she had been getting me ready for today.

I had come home without any heroic business on my mind, without plans to help her ready herself for dying, without thoughts about reconciliation. I had come for no other reason than to be with her, alone. Months earlier, Ellisene had brought Mom from Hamburg up to Little Rock to my brother's house and left her there for a week or so. Flying down from New York, I had looked forward to a weekend with her and Willard's family, but as it turned out, I felt uneasy most of the time. Saturday night I took everyone to dinner. I thought it would be a treat for Mom. She had always liked to dress up, eat out, put on the dog a bit, especially in Little Rock, the only city we could claim that seemed a little bigger than life. This time, though, she was morose, withdrawn. We had no time to talk privately, no time at dinner or elsewhere to give and take from each other what we needed. There in Little Rock someone else dictated the terms, and that made all the difference. She reacted as she always did when things didn't go her way, retreating inside herself, pouting. No one could outdo her on that score.

Just before I had to leave for the airport on Sunday, she and I went out on the front porch by ourselves. We held each other and cried. I don't remember a thing we said, but I remember thinking that I had been wrong: it would not be our last visit. She seemed strong in her frailty, wide-eyed and alert, even though she wasn't smiling much, wasn't asking her usual probing questions. Those questions about my happiness or about Ann or about Patrick and Tim were never simple ones. She expected to be let into our lives, no holds barred. And I had learned over the years that I couldn't tell her too much or she'd meddle, offering irritating advice. She wasn't so much trying to stir up trouble as she was testing my loyalty. She wanted some confirmation of her own influence in my life. After sizing me up on the outside, she went for the heart. But this time she hadn't tried to pry me open.

Her own life had whittled itself down to bare bones: a succession of days in a nursing home; daily, obligatory visits from Ellisene; not even a room of her own. Pretty dismal stuff on the whole, but she bore up fairly well. The family pictures were there, her favorite chair (a gift from Willard), sunshine, flowers, a tree outside the window, a telephone, and a steady stream of visitors bringing back to her what she had always given them: acceptance and wise counsel. For over forty-five years, they had come to her in that little bus station of hers, and she had imposed only one condition on her generosity: they had better not try to hoodwink her. She could see behind their eyes to the truth. And they knew it. Whatever she gave them lasted.

At my thirty-year high school reunion about a year after Mom died, we began, at Ross Bryant's prompting, to tell each other stories about friends and teachers—Mrs. Agnes Etheridge, Miss Olive Smith, Mr. Sheets—and stories about Mr. Portis, our superintendent who had come across from Alabama to southeast Arkansas with what we thought of as a strange accent. On that reunion night, Fred Sivils still had him down perfect, could say "woirk" just right, could even remember Mr. Portis's hands, the way he pressed his fingers together as he spoke to us in assembly, telling us as he leaned into the microphone, "You've got to 'woirk' hard if you're ever gonna 'ccomplish anything." For over three hours that evening, first one and then another of us recalled embarrassing moments, told tales of meanness, conjured up stories of occasional generosity. We babbled like school children, reentering the past as if there had been no intervening years, casting aside whatever we thought we had become—simply because Ross bid us talk.

At the end of the evening, Ross told a story of his own. He was the funniest guy in the class, so I expected him to join Fred Sivils and Herbert Wallace in some scathing attack that would rip open yet another curtain on those earlier days. But quite uncharacteristically, he began on a serious note. "It was in 1969," he said, "when I went to I-ran. There was a guy there named John Towery. Towery was the office manager. He came from somewhere around Swartz, Louisiana, down close to Monroe.

And he had a friend drove a bus for Trailways. He'd been up to Hamburg with this friend several times. When I got to that construction job over in I-ran, Towery was the second guy I talked to. 'You're from Hamburg, Arkansas, huh?' he asked when I walked into his office.

"Yeah, I sure am," Ross said.

"Do you by any chance know Miss Nan Jo Hoy who runs the bus station?"

At that moment, Ross said he felt like he hadn't come very far from home. He had known Mom all his life. So had most everyone else who lived in Ashley County, and so had many others who spent no more than a few hours waiting for a connection as they made their way across country or traveled from one end of the state to the other. She did her mothering there on those old slat benches, and many of those she took time with kept coming back over the years. A kid from New York, who must have looked pretty destitute, came through during the war. Mom gave him and a friend a room at our house for something short of a week, fed them, and then sent them on their way to California. Years later, long after the war, a fellow pulled up in front of the station in a "Cadillac a block long," she said, and brought her a case of the finest Scotch whiskey money could buy. No matter that she never touched the stuff, she was thrilled. Hal Kanter, on the way up, was writing scripts and screenplays. Over the years, they corresponded, and she watched for his name to show up in the credits at the end of television shows. When it did, she'd write a note. Sometimes he sent letters back. She saved one that came when she was eighty. He wrote of "how very long ago it was that we first met in that sweet town—in a less sophisticated and certainly far more pleasant era.... The years have ... never dimmed the glow of your hospitality and encouragement." He thanked her and "other Hamburg folks who were so kind to a young kid with a dream."

At West Point, my Pennsylvania roommate had a hankering

to date a movie starlet. He looked down his nose at my feeble southern beginnings, figuring that coming east had occasioned my first pair of shoes. He and a friend from Boston used to razz me about meeting their dates; they wanted their eastern girls to hear me talk. With Mom's friend Hal Kanter in the back of my mind, I bet my roommate a dinner in New York City that I could beat him to a starlet. Mom covered my bet and called Kanter for help. He had written the screenplay for an Elvis Presley movie, and a young actress named Dolores Hart who had been in the movie was doing a play with Cornelia Otis Skinner and George Peppard in New York. Kanter came through, and the feat made my yearbook, overshadowing whatever else I managed to do in those four years. Mom laughed over the victory from afar.

As I sat by her bed in the nursing home that day, I yearned to look as far back into life as we could go. I had come to be with her one last time, alone. But I had come with pen and paper in hand. I wanted her to tell me things about her family, about my dad, about her life, that she had always been private about. I wanted to get something down on paper. I imagine now that I was desperate without knowing it, trying to find a way to hold on to her forever with no idea how to do it. I wanted her help, but looking at her sunk in the pillows, I didn't think she'd be able to take me very far. I even wondered if we'd be able to talk. As I sat there waiting for her to come back to me, writing gave way to remembering, and the little boy in my head took over.

Outside the bus station, when I was five, I learned that my father had left home. My sister and two of her friends were comforting Mom as we sat together in the 1943 sedan. Scampering over the front seat into the back, I was stunned by her grief. It was my first sense of a woman in need, my first sense of trauma and conflict, a rare moment in my early life when Mom allowed me to have access to suffering of any kind. She never complained about his leaving; she always looked back on ten glorious years of loving, that's how on very rare occasions she referred to life with my dad. But there was a bitter end, I suspect, even if she chose to ignore it. A letter written on U.S. Army Air Forces stationery from Seymour Johnson Field, North Carolina, on October 8, 1943, closes this way: "And mom I want you to stick to that bus station and if he will sell out at $3,000 take it even if you have to close it up. Don't pay $7,000 cause its half yours to begin with." It was from Dub, my half-brother, in training for a job as a tail gunner on a B-26. I found the letter forty-two years later in a dresser drawer where she kept her most prized possessions: gifts of words, letters of encouragement, things of value to the heart.

She and my dad had obviously had something special, something very special. They owned almost a city block—service station, bus station, hardware and furniture store. And they had built it from nothing. She had married him a widow with three children, trying to make ends meet on whatever was left from her first marriage to a man who had died young of cancer before anyone knew what cancer was. He had left her a house in town, an adjacent lot, and a forty-acre farm on the outskirts where they raised hay and she later grew trees following the good advice of friends who worked for the Crossett Company.

Pat Hoy was the marshal's son, from good enough stock to be in the local history books, and he must have been a sight for sore eyes. The pictures don't tell the whole story, but they're not bad. My favorite one has me standing between his legs in front of the service station. I've got a four-year-old's look of determination written all over my face, disgusted I imagine from the picture-taking. He has his hands resting on my shoulders, and my arms are curled up as if I might be flexing my muscles. But I'm not. I'm pouting. My wrists curl over his and I'm holding on to him desperately while trying to pull out of the picture. He is ramrod straight, his eyes behind sunglasses, his shirt sleeves rolled halfway up bulging muscles. The relaxed power of his arms matches the power of his neck. He looks like he could hold the world up without straining. I can see what Elizabeth Hoy meant a few years ago when my cousin Robert kept interrupting her after I walked into a room full of people, seeing that part of the family for the first time in over twenty years. From across the room, Robert kept trying to get Elizabeth to acknowledge how much I looked like my dad. Finally she looked up from her conversation and announced her findings to a whole room of relatives. "Yes," she said, "he does look like Pat, but he's not nearly as handsome."

I can sense his strength in what I like to imagine as their wedding picture. They're in each other's arms standing on a road bridge; I expect they're on the way to something special. In all my life, I never saw her look that happy. I have to imagine the colors, but its pretty clear she's in a blue voile dress with polka dots about the size of quarters. If I'm not mistaken it hung in her closet the rest of her life. She's wearing white lace-up heels, spiffy looking shoes. He's in a white shirt, tie, vest (already out of his coat), baggy pants with cuffs, and soft dress shoes. He's half a head taller and in command even as he leans them back into the railing; she's floating it seems, only one foot on the ground. She's thirty-eight; he's twenty. The marriage license lists twenty-five and twenty. Not much discernible difference in age in the picture. Whatever they had lasted ten years. At the end, she had me and two of her other children, and all in the way of holdings that she had before he came along . . . plus a bus station. She also had self-respect and standing in a community where standards of propriety didn't leave much margin for error. I imagine most folks had given the marriage about six months. It ended with memories so sacred she wouldn't talk about them even to me more than forty years later. What the station cost her in money I don't know, but it became our home; we went to the house mostly for sleeping and eating.

Inside the bus station, I knew only joy. Even now, I look back at a bottoms-up six year old hanging precariously over the edge of a cardboard box searching for treasures: toy trucks, precious ball bearings, a German bayonet my brother had sent home from England where he flew weekly into the flak of war, his medals, everyone's old letters, pictures, assorted scraps of family history. We were there beside each other, as she sold Trailways bus tickets to droves of people going to Detroit, Shreveport, New Orleans, Gary . . . people setting out for a harvest of treasures the black dirt of Arkansas couldn't provide. I needed no other treasures for myself during those carefree days, had no sense at all that someday the idyll would have to end. I played there in the sheltered space of that office between the white waiting room in front and the colored in back. Under the high counters, in and around the boxes, I'd hide out until she called me to pack a box of treats for long-distance passengers. Way up high, up there on top of the counters, I made my journey round the glass jars surrounding our kingdom, careful not to drop the rattling big lids as I reached in for the goodies: Tom's peanuts, cheese crackers, pork skins, round-the-worlds, peanut planks, Baby Ruths, Snickers. Hersheys too. Each passenger also got a cold drink that I fished from the icy waters of the "Co-Cola" box—a Dr. Pepper, a Coke, a NuGrape.

As she struggled to put her own life in order, I had no sense of her burdens or the one she was asking me to carry. I had no understanding of the love she was giving me, its inherent obligations, its power to limit and to fructify. I know only that I grew up secure in the fact that I was loved and cared for, never having to wonder if there was a place to turn when I needed comfort, never once having to suffer the agony of loneliness. Some would say, and did, that she loved me too much. But I've begun to doubt their judgment, just as I've begun to doubt most of the psychology that makes of the mother too little or too much, whether she be nurturing or devouring, whether she be the Great Mother or my very own. Her complexity fascinates me, pulls me in and pushes me away. Going back to her, leaving her, returning again and again, remains the fundamental, basic pattern of my life—my pearl of great price.

The facing walls of Mom's office carried the whole story. On the outside wall above a massive oak desk with the cash register on it, she had a bank of shelves, each flanked with family pictures. The shelves held boxes of plug tobacco, Prince Albert, Zig Zag cigarette papers, B.C. headache powders, Bull Durham, Lucky Strikes, Chesterfields, Kleenex, Tums, handkerchiefs, assorted odds and ends for travelers—and there on the shelves, with those simple necessities and the little writing pads she used for keeping informal notes about who owed her what, were the pictures. Ellisene, Willard, Dub, and I were there, of course, her offspring from two marriages. But there were many others. When I came back over the years she would tell me, when I asked, about the new faces, the new bus drivers, their wives and kids, a young high school boy or girl who had dropped by for healing conversation over the years and had included a picture along with the graduation invitation. The new faces reminded me that her life was going on without me, that I wasn't altogether a part of it. She was battling loneliness in her own way.

On the inside wall, above the Western Union telegraph machine, were what seemed like a thousand little cubby holes, full of short tickets, message forms, schedules—opportunities for folks to connect with another world. To the left of the printer table and at a right angle to it was what I now think of as a giant writing desk with a slanting top, but she didn't use it as a work space; inside its storage bins she kept stacks of longer tickets and the large three-ring notebooks that contained the scheduling and routing secrets. Above the storage compartments, on the back upright shelf, I could scramble up to encounter Captain

Marvel, Superman, *Life, True Romance* (if I dared). On the wall just to the right of the telegraph machine, she had a Trailways map of the United States. When I studied it, I could make all the routes come to Hamburg or make all of them lead away. I spent a lot of time up on a stool keeping track of where people were going.

On the counter facing the front of the station, she did her major work. That's where she wrote the tickets. That's where she kept the rubber stamps with the names of towns and cities where people living in Hamburg and down in the swamp towns (Parkdale, Wilmot, Montrose) wanted to travel. As I grew up, I spent lots of time up on that counter where she'd let me play with the stamps and pens, making my mark first on scraps of paper and later on the tickets themselves. There in that station, we were partners. At first I was just a stamper, but as she brought my mind and my imagination to life, I found my own way through the schedule books and began answering the telephone to tell people she was busy and would call them back.

She gave me work to do, and the bus drivers fathered me; they all took rest stops in Hamburg. It was their watering hole, not because it was a scheduled stop but because Mom was there. Watson helped me build my model airplanes; Brown taught me how to be 6'2", weigh 220 pounds, and be gentle as a baby and powerful as a bear; Parnell gave me insight into courage; he was a bus driver from the right side of the tracks with enough gumption to do what he wanted to do; and Duchaine, the Cajun, gave me early glimpses into language and bayou culture. All of the special ones had keys to the station so they could leave packages at night if Mom decided not to meet the late buses. The drivers came in, had a Coke, made change for passengers needing refreshments, and usually left a note with the money that was always there the next morning. All of those men who were still alive came back for her funeral.

I looked at her there in the bed that day and saw it all. She didn't have to help very much. She was in my head, and I began to see sitting there in her chair that she always would be. Thinking about her and scratching out notes, I noticed her moving a bit, and as she opened her eyes, she started to speak.

"I want to know about the boys," she says, gasping for air to create words.

I tell her.

"Tell them to stay in there and pitch 'til the last minute, you hear."

"I will, Mom. You know I will. Do you remember when Patrick drove down to see you a few months ago?" Her face lights up, and she smiles again, even pushes herself up a bit with her elbows.

"Ooo," she says gathering strength, "he took me for a ride in that convertible, around the square, with the top down. He's something else. I felt like Marilyn Monroe." She cackles a bit and looks up at me with a gleam in her eye.

"Tim sends his love, wishes he could be here," I say to her.

"I know, honey," she says. "He sent me a card, over yonder in the drawer," she continues, pointing me over to it. "Get it out for me, will you?" I do, and she holds it for a minute. "Don't forget to tell them what I said. They've got to keep plugging along, you know?"

Her words rattled from a life riddled with losses enough to stop Coxey's army, but she was still hanging on, struggling. Nevertheless there was the usual undercurrent of uncertainty, a question still riding on her own advice. She'd always invested herself in her own words, and even at that moment, especially at that moment, she wanted to be reassured, comforted. Though I knew it was time to meet her on her own terms again, I hesitated, resisted, as I began to hear her words from other times rising in my head: *What can't be cured must be endured, honey; where there's a will there's a way.* Watching me, she knew I had been listening to her, knew too that as I looked away and made cryptic notes, I read her like a book. Her advice was never altogether simple, never free. Again, I sensed that she wanted confirmation that I put her first, above everything else in my life.

"Mom, do you have a word for Ann?" I ask.

"Ann Veazey?"

"No, Mom, my Ann. Ann Hoy," I insist, wondering whether we're headed for conflict or whether she's just too tired to pay attention. But she snaps back to life again.

"Oh, your Ann. I think she's great! You tell her so for me, you hear."

Theirs had been more than the inevitable testy relationship between a mother and her son's young wife. I was the fair-haired, only child of that second marriage. In her mind I had been sent to take Dub's place after he was killed in the Battle of the Bulge. Never mind that I had been there all along. She got the premonition in a dream she told me, and she stopped grieving. Dub had been her favorite, and when the message came from the War Department that his B-26 was missing, she chose to believe in the miraculous possibility that he would someday come home, instead of believing in the stark reality of a flak-infested sky over Germany. She pursued that dream until another more palpable one came along, this one presumably from God. Although she went to church all her life and saw to it that everyone else in her family did, I never thought of her as a God-fearing woman. But she was tough and presumptuous. Her pipeline to the top was direct. Make no mistake about it. The dream confirmed it, and I became the agent of her salvation.

Until I turned out to be a different man from the one she was sure she had created, our lives were as idyllic as any two lives could be. She saw in me the fulfillment of all her dreams and told me so often. But she was neither a clutching mother nor an interfering one as I grew up. And I always saw my life apart from hers. I understood even as a teenager that she had her life invested in me, yet her expectations didn't seem much of a burden. She, like Mr. Portis, had taught me about hard work, and my successes seemed strangely impersonal. They belonged more to effort than to me. Winning an award was not the occasion for strutting in public. My greatest joy came from making Mom happy; the grades, the scout work, the athletic awards were not nearly as important as her reaction to them. So public ceremony never meant as much to me as a private moment of sharing.

I marvel even today that she sent me off to West Point, put me on a bus with a friend from Warren, Arkansas, setting us off in search of our own dreams. I thought for a long time that she had sent me to redeem herself, but I have to measure that notion against the risk she certainly knew she was taking. She put me up to leaving; she turned me loose, helped me see beyond good opportunities much closer to home. She sent me off to become a soldier, knowing full well what that meant.

Later, even my choice of a wife suited her. Few of my girlfriends had. With Ann, she liked what she saw. Ann was one of us. I hadn't married either the Jewish girl or the Catholic; hadn't even married an easterner after four years in New York. There had been some close calls in her mind and one or two in mine, but to find a red-haired, Scotch-Irish woman who was also a Methodist—well even mother-love had to make room for that . . . for awhile.

It took over ten years for the battle flags to go up, but during the meantime I deluded myself into thinking that I could satisfy both of them. Distance was on my side; we weren't in Hamburg very often, and Mom was only in our house once a year. When she was, she didn't let things sit long before she started probing and interfering. Initially both Ann and I let it ride.

But then Mom became unbearable. She was pretty astute about waiting for moments of family conflict to do her number. Pout and innuendo were her weapons. The pattern, no matter what the occasion, was always the same. She'd sit around and watch us for a few days until she found something suspicious about the way we lived our lives. In the beginning her complaints generally had to do with the children. We ought to give them more freedom, she said. We ought to let them stay up late just this once; it wouldn't hurt. I, she told me, ought to talk to Patrick; he was unhappy. His mother was being a little tough on him. She'd tell Patrick too, the four year old. Then I would be in the middle. She even sent advice books back through the mail, marked up devotionals, so we wouldn't miss her point.

When she sensed that I wasn't listening or heeding her advice, she became relentless as she tried to worm her way into our marriage. She wanted a part of it. One night during one of her visits to West Point, we had friends over for dinner. I decided not to forgo the wine just because she was there. When I uncorked the bottle, she winced. The next day, when I went home to have lunch with her, she asked me to tell her again why Ann and I had been over to the Superintendent's house three days earlier. I told her we had been "house stuffers." The General needed Colonels to talk to guests; we all had to take our turns. She wasn't convinced by the truth and suggested instead that I must have been in some kind of trouble. She figured maybe I'd been drinking a little too much. It followed of course, in her mind, that the Superintendent of the U.S. Military Academy had called me and Ann over for counseling. Never mind that I was forty-four. To her way of thinking, Mom had lost a husband to the bottle, and she was doing her dead-level best not to lose a son.

INSTINCT FOR SURVIVAL

It was pretty uncomfortable being caught between the love of two women, each of them expecting me to be absolutely loyal to their notions of me. For about ten years, I had tried to meet their expectations, unreasonable as I thought they were. When we were in our separate houses, I ignored the problem, refused to talk about it. When we were together, I tried diplomacy and accommodation. Nothing worked.

I know now that the real problem was the woman in my head and that woman had been formed under the influence of my mother. So motherly-love and wifely-love warred in my imagination, and I wasn't reflective enough at the time to see that I was coming home from my corporate job everyday expecting to meet my mother at the side door. My greatest satisfaction during those early years of marriage came from the adoring, stroking corporation. Within it, I was everyone's favorite. No need to elicit praise; I had it. But I wanted more. I wanted to go home to a woman who had been teaching school, cleaning diapers, washing dishes, buying groceries—and reexperience bliss. But I had married a spitfire woman and neither my silence nor my pouting could subdue her. She had no intention of matching the woman in my head, and when she announced (way ahead of her time) that she needed *space* and that I needed to move into an Army BOQ, the bottom fell out of my life . . . for the first time. At thirty-six the idyll ended, and I walked out of my house into another world.

Stunned, I prolonged the struggle for a few months, trying still to split my loyalty. Finally, I walked into a phone booth in Oklahoma on a hot, sweltering July morning and told Mom to stop meddling, told her especially to stop interfering with my efforts to save my troubled marriage. I had vows of my own to keep.

I broke her heart and knew it. The letter I wrote afterward was in her special dresser drawer; only three of the hundreds I had written over the years were there. Even now, I like what I said, and she did too or she wouldn't have kept the letter. She understood yet showed no signs of forgiveness for over a decade. She simply set the hurt aside over the years and rejoined us cautiously after Ann and I got our family together again. I became ever more private over the years, refusing to talk to Mom about my happiness or my sorrow. The limits I established deprived her of what she wanted most to know.

At Mom's bedside, I finally hear a note of accommodation in her greeting for Ann. She's come a long distance on her own. The flags are down, and I can tell she means what she says. Although her voice struggles and her body fights her, her composure is more perfect than it has ever been in my memory. She's no longer threatened.

"Now," she says, looking straight into my tearful eyes, "we've got to find a way to get around to talking about this whatchamadoodle."

It's a word I'd heard all my life. But I'd never heard her use it. Today, though, I know instantly its meaning. "Don't you think we're already talking about the whatchamadoodle?" I ask.

She smiles.

We talk for a long time, saying what we have to say in indirect ways until finally she is fairly sure of my answer to the one question she still wants to ask. She senses that now, after my long, seasoned marriage, two sons, yet another war, too much education, and all the small changes and failures, nothing has made a whit of difference between us.

"I want to know," she asks, "if you still love me?"

Looking into those unblinking eyes, I know a simple yes will not do. She wants nourishment. The mouth below those eyes moves with a slight but constant twitch, the body's pain betraying her, but her mind and her eyes are steady.

"Mom"—my voice cracks as I struggle to give my life back

to her—"everything follows from what you gave me in the beginning. I'm always the kid at the bus station, always watching what you were doing there, remembering the way you kept loving despite the losses. You gave me the gift. You know that, don't you?"

"I thought so, but a lot's happened."

"Yeah, you're right, but we have to go away. We come and go. Men do. We have no choice."

When I turned away from her to Ann, she persisted, as she often did against all odds, to demand what I could not always give her and still survive. I want to tell her we can't stay in that childlike state all our lives, being nurtured, loved, protected, if we are to have lives of our own. Neither can we return to the folds later, unchanged. But only minutes before, she has warned me not to get too studious about my life. So I hold my tongue, wondering if she knows that we have to keep coming back, in whatever state, to the source.

"Will Patrick come back?" she asks.

"I think Patrick knows now how much we all love him. He'll be slow coming round, but he'll be fine. So will Tim; he's about to break away. Don't worry about them. Just remember one thing for me, okay? They think you're special."

"Do they really? Tell 'em what I told you, you hear? Tell 'em to keep pitching, not to give up."

"I will. I'll tell them. Now, about the whatchamadoodle, have we about covered that?"

"I think so."

"Okay, Mom, would you like to close your eyes and rest a bit, or do you want some more peas and squash?"

"No, I'm fine," she whispered. "You go see your sister and come back later."

Smiling, she closed her eyes and squeezed my hand. I hugged her neck, kissed her, and said goodbye.

GOINGS AND COMINGS

I DID NOT see her again after that visit. But on a warm September morning among the headstones, we celebrated, remembering her. She had left so little undone during her ninety years there was no need for mourning.

I still go back on occasion to visit my sister, and while I'm there, I take great pleasure that our house next door has been moved across town and that there is only space where we once slept and ate. The bus station has been demolished to make way for a parking lot for the Methodist church. She knew about that before she died. Made no difference. She had actually ended her days in the station at eighty-five during a tornado, hunkered under the old oak desk until Ellisene's husband rescued her from the torrential rains that came in the aftermath of destruction. She had been spared she would say. Much of the roof had been ripped off. My scrapbooks, many of the pictures, lots of the papers had been ruined. But now I see that nothing had actually been lost. I am still grounded to that place, and I know that when I choose to return to her, I can do so at my bidding—whether in time of need or in time of joy.

Recently, when I returned home for a short visit, we were gathered at my sister's house. Sitting down at the supper table, my niece turned quietly to me and said, "I've been talking to her a lot lately. I wish I could see her just one more time."

"I talk to her too," I said, "but I don't think I need to see her. At times though, I can hardly stand it."

The next day on the way out of town, I stopped by the cemetery. The mid-morning sun warmed me as I lowered my head to look over my bifocals. The numbers framing her life—1895–1985—seemed strangely magical to me as a caressing breeze stirred the hair up and down my neck and whistled around my ears. I listened to the wind's music, listened to the words rising in my head, and tried for a few moments to give her substance. I thanked her only for the gift of feeling and turned to walk back toward my son's car, parked along the edge of grass beyond a corridor of headstones.

As I turned away from her yet again, I knew I would be back. And even as I left, I discovered that she was still with me, in my head, stirring my spirit, reminding me that nothing, absolutely nothing, could ever rip us asunder.

Mosaics of Southern Masculinity

Nobody under forty can believe how nearly everything's *inherited.*
REYNOLDS PRICE

HE SIMPLY WASN'T THERE. My sister and two of her friends were comforting my mom as we sat out front of our bus station in the 1943 sedan. As I scampered over the front seat into the back, I was stunned by her grief. It caught me in midair, and as I toppled into the space between Ellisene and Dot, I stopped my squirming and snuggled down deep. He was gone, and he wouldn't be back. They were trying to help her through the ordeal, trying to stop the heaving and the suffering. And even though their words made no sense to me, I could feel her loss in my five-year-old bones. He was gone.

I saw him occasionally for brief periods over the next twenty-four years, but when he died at fifty-six of cirrhosis of the liver, I had not known him. I had no cause to miss him until I was thirty-five and it seemed my own marriage wouldn't survive. I missed him again at forty-three when Patrick left for college, and I began to wonder if I had done enough for him and his younger brother Tim, began to rummage around in my memories recalling signs of my father's influence, began, for the first time, to try to assemble a mosaic of my own masculinity.

I MUST HAVE BEEN SEVEN or eight, sitting at my desk on the sleeping porch, working under the glare of a hanging light bulb, when my half-brother, home on furlough, walked through the room and stopped to watch me do my arithmetic. I was absorbed in the figuring and could hear only the thud and soft glide of the iron as Mom touched up her dress for work. After a few minutes Willard interrupted me.

"Make a five again."

"Huh?"

"Make a five."

I made one. Starting at the bottom of the half-circle, I moved the pencil around counter-clockwise to the top of the curve, made a short vertical line straight up and moved the lead point to the right completing the horizontal bar, all without ever lifting my pencil from the paper. One smooth, natural motion. Easy. A five from the bottom up.

"Look at this, Mother," he exclaimed, obviously beside himself. "Have you ever seen Butch make a five? Pat Hoy! No one but Pat Hoy makes a five like that!"

I didn't understand his excitement, but I remembered the moment—my first conscious memory of my dad's influence, all the more interesting to me now because I know he didn't teach me to make fives. Neither did Miss Culbertson, nor Miss Barnes, nor any of my other teachers. It was a genetic remnant that came along with his smile lines, his love of fast cars, and his damning fascination with women. I knew none of this at seven.

The last time I drove Mom from Hamburg to Little Rock, she was eighty-five. I was forty-two. We had just left Monticello heading north for Star City, and I was stuck behind a log truck and a couple of straggling cars. When an opening came, I made my move, whizzed past the three vehicles, and eased back into my lane as a southbound eighteen-wheeler breezed by. I turned to Mom with a smile breaking on my face.

"Pat Hoy!" she said.

"What?"

"I've seen him do it a thousand times."

"Do what?"

"Turn to me with that look and a grin from ear to ear, wait'n for approval."

Three years later, in the fall of the year, I was at Fort Leonard Wood, Missouri, with two younger Army officers. After two hard days of trying to teach high-ranking civil servants and senior officers to write more effectively, we needed sustenance. Leonard Wood had only a steak-and-fries restaurant on the strip and a small night club. We opted first for the mediocre food and then on a whim drove across the highway to the honky-tonk. We had spent six summer weeks with our traveling word show, laughing our way through airports, making students laugh while they learned in the classroom. We had a fairly good sense of each other's daytime habits. At nights we had gone our separate ways, visiting friends at each of the posts, Army life being very much a small-town experience. The communities were separate, spread all over the world, but nonetheless of a piece. I was never a stranger in any one of them.

Our favorite pastime during the previous summer had been a Jungian game. We tried to second-guess each other's taste in women, tried to guess the nature of the woman in the other man's head. It was a game of images. We tried to predict "grid overlap," guessing when the woman in the classroom or the airport or on the plane would match the imagined woman in one of our buddy's heads. We joked about "anima seizures": spellbinding image overlap. The game was an older man's contribution to the summer fun.

The club across the street from the restaurant was small and close, but it felt friendly when we walked in in our khakis, polo shirts, and docksiders. The Missouri cowboys paid no attention, but the waitress seemed amused when she brought the beers. A Willie Nelson number drew couples out into the hazy space of the dance floor where refracting lights played softly around cowboy hats and occasionally found a patch of sequined hair. A strapping, lithe woman and her little man caught my eye. They were feeling their way around the floor, lost in the rhythms of those "lonely, lonely times."

Before I knew it, one of my buddies was on the floor, cutting in. The little man went back to his table, sat down, and tilted his hat forward just a bit. He sat with his back to us, but I could see him hook the heels of his boots over the bottom rung of the chair, slightly defiant.

The woman seemed unaware that she had changed partners. When she went back to the table, her man continued to stare at the door.

THE VOCALIST didn't sound much like Anne Murray, but when she launched into "Son of a Rotten Gambler," I knew I couldn't sit there drinking beer any longer. I walked over to the strapping woman and asked her if she'd like to dance.

Reaching for my hand, she said, "I'd really like to, but I can't."

I asked her why not.

"He doesn't want me to dance with anyone else."

I looked over at him, sitting there immobilized, still staring at the front door. He might not have moved for three songs. They hadn't danced again. So I moved between them.

"Would you mind if I danced with your friend?" I asked, feeling my way into the protocol.

He didn't move his eyes.

"Look," I said pulling up a stool from the table behind us, "I'm not after your woman. I just want to dance this song with her."

He cleared his throat but kept up his business with the door.

She reached up and put her hand on my arm, pulling me down in her direction as she said, "I'm sorry. I really would like to dance, but I can't do it tonight."

I made it back to our table as the singer slid into the last stanza: "He'd be the son of his father / His father the teacher." But the teacher wasn't there to ask. I wondered what he would have done, wondered what the honky-tonk rules called for?

I remember his stopping by our house late one afternoon when I was about thirteen; he was on the way out of town, on the move as usual. I could smell vodka over Dentyne. Mom asked him where he was headed.

"Juking."

"Where to?"

"Chula."

I didn't know where Chula was, but I guessed it was the Howdy Club in El Dorado, miles away over the dump, a long stretch of suspended roadway surrounded on both sides by the Ouachita river. I expected him to die there. But in those days, his life seemed charmed. Chula, I now suspect, was Xanadu. It was there he built his "dome of pleasure," there he "drunk the milk of Paradise." And perhaps, like me, as he listened to the "woman wailing," he "heard from far/Ancestral voices." I felt close to him that night in Missouri, very close, felt him in my bones again. And I felt too a painful advantage. He didn't have the wherewithal to distinguish the woman in his head from the one outside. Seizures carried him through life, and when his charms wore out, his liver couldn't carry the load.

The next morning at the post exchange, I saw the strapping woman. The image had dissipated; it couldn't hold up under the light of day. But she held up quite well. She apologized again, said her man had had a hard day, said he wasn't usually like that, said he was a good man. She thanked me for letting them be the night before. I liked her, liked my dad. I think he would have left the cowboy alone too. He was good at that, leaving people alone. Until that morning, it had never seemed a virtue.

When my father began to reappear in my imagination, I turned to Erich Neumann for clarification. He claims that all of us have two fathers (as well as two mothers), one actual, the other archetypal, spiritual—a collective Father. Sons, in the decidedly patriarchal psychology of Neumann's *Origins and History of Consciousness,* must overcome both of the World Parents and both of the actual parents in order to gain independence and reach maturity. The son-hero initially fears the threat to "the spiritual, masculine principle," fears "being swallowed by the maternal unconscious," and needs help at the outset from the fathers. Because I had shut my real father out of my life and out of my imagination for so long, he was no help to me as a youngster. What independence I gained from the Mothers, I gained at the hands of the town Fathers who saw to my upbringing in a small southern hamlet that bears even today the indelible stamp of masculinity.

Neumann tells us " 'The fathers' are the representatives of law and order, from the earliest taboos to the most modern judicial systems; they hand down the highest values of civilization, whereas the mothers control the highest, i.e., deepest, values of life and nature." Those gender differences ring true of my experience. The collective voice, the voice of the fathers there in that little hamlet called Hamburg, said this: you will be in the Boy Scouts; you will play football; you will go on the hunt; you will expose yourself to trials so that you can test your strength and independence; you will be a man and uphold the institutional values (never mind our own waywardness; what we represent, not what we do, that's what's important). The deepest voices said something different: you will be a gentle man; you will go to church; you will love and honor your mother and father (even if he has deserted you); you will avoid conflict and danger; you will remain always loyal to us, the deepest voices; you will never abandon us.

But there were ironic inconsistencies. The town fathers held up only part of their bargain. They understood too little of the myth they were unconsciously enacting. They pushed me into tests but did not draw me into community. My time on the hunt was limited to a day at a time, no weekends, no continuity, no time for fellowship. They forced Mom to let me play football, not because they were concerned about my development but because I was fairly tough and wiry; they wanted a winning team. The scouting activities were more satisfying; the men looked after our development. They drew all of us together, gave us their time and their guidance, took us in the woods, took us west to a national jamboree in California, taught us teamwork and responsibility. But always, at the end of those activities, the scoutmasters went home with their own sons. I could never confirm the experience, after the fact, with a man. The rituals never claimed me entirely. But, of course, no one knew anything was missing. I certainly didn't.

There was yet another irony at work in my life long before I was aware of it. It was my mother, not my father, who sent me off to West Point, off to war—the same woman who, sending two sons to an earlier world war, had lost one. I keep wondering, even today, whether she was seduced by the spell of the old romance, unable to see the irony of what she was doing. Did she send me away to assuage those other losses? I'll never know for sure. But I sense, even now years after her death, a touch of madness in the way she and other women send men off to war with their blessings—their own heads swimming with visions of grandeur. My mother was not at all clearheaded about West Point and the other side of soldiering.

Virginia Woolf was. In *Mrs. Dalloway* she mocks Peter Walsh, exposing his infantile urge to be "an adventurer," a "romantic buccaneer." To remind us of the danger of following such urges, Woolf has Walsh cross paths with Septimus Warren Smith, a young man who has been left crazed by war. Against the comic story of Peter's heroism, we hear the tragic story of how Septimus left home "a mere boy" to go up to London, leaving behind him "an absurd note . . . such as great men have written, and the world has read later when the story of their struggles has become famous."

But, of course, Septimus does not become a great man. Compelled and inspired by his teacher Miss Isabel Pole—who "lent him books, wrote him scraps of letters," in general fed his active male imagination with "vanity, ambition, idealism, passion, loneliness, courage, laziness, the usual seeds"—Septimus becomes "one of the first to volunteer." He goes to war "to save an England which consisted almost entirely of Shakespeare's plays and Miss Isabel Pole in a green dress walking in a square." Having gone, "he developed manliness; he was promoted." But while there, Septimus lost his mind; having lost it, he gained insight that made him no longer fit to live in the culture that had sent him out to serve.

Of a different generation from Septimus, I felt no deep yearning for the sound of the guns when I left my mom and that community in south Arkansas. My manliness had already been tempered by the deeper values. Lead soldiers and toy cannons, "Dixie" and rebel flags had not moved my spirit. I had built my model airplanes in youth to commemorate the loss of my brother, one of the war's turret gunners. Had I been born a decade later, I might, like my friend Sam Pickering, have decorated my model planes with flowers. But I came after the romance of the Old South, after the other great wars too—and before the flower children. My mind's irony blossomed in a war foreign to all who had served before me.

When I left the South, I was certain it had not claimed me. I left under the impress of an active male imagination—young and naive, my head full of grandeur. I was looking for a way to loose the ties that bound me to family and region. I wanted independence, wanted to be cut loose, turned out on my own.

Susceptible to an urge deeper than any particular war could command, I was oblivious to the consequences of where I was going. A romance far older than even the South was claiming me. I sought only the challenge and the promise. West Point offered me a way into the world of the fathers. But it was a gauntlet cast into my path by an adoring mother.

YEARS LATER, after Vietnam, after my own father's death, when I finally turned my mind South again, I began to understand what Allen Tate meant in "A Southern Mode of the Imagination" about the change that took place after World War I, the change that turned the southern mind inward, causing it to "shift from rhetoric to dialectic," creating what he later characterized as a "literature of introspection" rather than a "literature of romantic illusion." I was not the "old Southern *rhetor*, the speaker who was eloquent before the audience but silent in himself." Rummaging around inside my head, I was discovering my heritage, recovering lost remnants of masculinity, developing a sense of irony fit for my experiences. By that time, I had slayed the Mothers and saved my marriage, knew enough Jung to be dangerous, and had begun to make peace with the woman in my head. She was occasionally helpful as I moved into middle age, and the stories I began to tell myself in order to live seemed mythic. They began to reach beyond me into the world. I sensed for the first time in my life that I could never be alone again.

In "A Lost Traveller's Dream," Tate writes of memory, her feminine nature, her free will. He writes of the difficulty of arresting the "flow of inner time." Memory, he says, has "its own life and purposes; it gives what *it* wills. . . . The latin *memoria* is properly a feminine noun, for women never forget; and likewise the soul is the *anima*, even in man, his vital principal and the custodian of memory, the image of woman that all men both pursue and flee." Tate reminds us too that the "imaginative writer is the archeologist of memory, dedicated to the minute particulars of the past, definite things—*prima sacrimenti memoria*. If his 'city' is to come alive again from a handful of shards, he will try to fit them together in an elusive jigsaw puzzle, most of the pieces of which are forever lost." By the time I read Tate's words, my life had already confirmed them, but they still give me consolation. They point the way into a deeper myth.

When Tate illustrates what he actually means by the southern myth, he relays the old story about the curse of slavery, the invasion from outside, the destruction of a culture. Myth is historical, a story imposed on a culture from the outside, a way of accounting for what happened, rather than a story that embodies a culture's sensibility. Working from the outside, imposing a story on events, Tate buries the more powerful, stabilizing story that has always been there in the images and activities of family life. Yet he too knew that other story, the one he tells in "The Fugitive" about the "simple homogeneous background . . . a sort of unity of feeling" that he and his friends took with them to the university. He's pointing to an inherent sensibility. The southern community itself was there before the war—masculine and feminine—the higher values of law and order underscored by the deeper values of life and nature.

A child of the matriarchy, I was raised on the South's deeper values. My sense of law and order, skewed by my sense of the foibles of actual men, caused me for years to undervalue the archetypal Father. I grew up in a house where dependence was more important than independence. So I grew up secure, seeing no need to hold my life together with stories of derring-do. Life was just fine until I moved out of that southern hamlet into the world of conflict—into the mania of competition, into war.

Yet the remnants of masculinity passed on by the town fathers served me well enough when I moved east and went, much later, to war. I carried to West Point and to Penn and to Vietnam a sense of community that had shaped my imagination without my knowing it. I had a survival kit but had no sense of its inherent ironies, complexities, contradictions, strengths. I would not begin to understand that inheritance fully until nearly thirty years later when I read Bill Berry's "Class Southerner." I was fifty. That essay gave me a sense of myself, a sense of what had made me different from almost all my northern friends. When I read literature or read the history books, I, like Bill, "wanted more than brilliance." I wanted "the fleshed body of a living past." I looked too for the story that formed around the words, the personal myth that shaped the writer's vision. I wanted meaning, wanted desperately to see how the stories I read illuminated the life I was trying to live.

Sitting here as I am, trying to fit the "handful of shards" together in the jigsaw puzzle that will constitute my own version of the city, I know that the masculine pieces are just now beginning to fit in place. Active all along, they have been influential in subtle ways. But my aversion to *machismo*—the boxing ring, the stench of the cadet gymnasium, the Army's insistence on masculine standards even when such standards are inappropriate—made me a maverick through my years of military service. Nevertheless, I stayed in the Army for almost three decades, stayed even when I had the chance and the inclination to leave. I think I was unwilling to turn the business of law and order over to the real men. They spend too much time building monuments to their own magnificence. They spend too much time in the gymnasium. They undervalue the deeper values.

IT TOOK ME YEARS to come face to face with my father. When I did, he was long dead. A number of people over the years had told me how much I looked like him, and scores of others had talked about how much they liked him, what a fine businessman he was. What they said was not meant to console me; they loved the man despite his faults, never qualifying their praise of him, never commenting about the drinking. He had won their hearts through warmth and generosity, a playful spirit, and just a touch of melancholy, I suspect. I sense it in myself, a bittersweet, desperate longing to be loved. All his friends told me how much he loved me; he never took the time.

Yet as I grew up I felt no need for consolation. I understood what had happened, where he had gone—his absence was one of the facts of my life. Part of my upbringing was to learn to live with that loss and to live without bitterness. I suspect that Mom's greatest accomplishment was keeping her mouth shut over her own deep loss; she engendered stability, protected me, and preserved the memory of their life together. She had a firm hold on the deeper values and so did most of the other people I grew up around. Those folks lived earnest lives, but they had a sense of humor, and they looked out for one another. Those of us who were fatherless got on with our lives, loved by mothers and other friends. The community was our family. So I had no reason to feel put out or left out because Pat Hoy had skipped town.

Nevertheless, as my children grew up, I made a simple, silent commitment: I would always be there. I knew nothing else to do. My memory afforded little help. Stories about my father gave me no pattern against which to measure life with my children. Ann had her own memories, and she often tried to turn me into her father. Whatever he had done with her, I was supposed to do with Patrick and Tim. I listened and abided when her suggestions made sense, but mostly I watched and waited for the children to need me. When they did, I tried to pay attention. What I know about fathering, they taught me.

Looking back on our life together, I think the teaching began in Oklahoma when it seemed that I would lose them, lose the opportunity to be there with them as they grew up. Work had become my salvation. There was certainly nothing malicious in my dedication. I had been trained to be a professional soldier. My mom had taught me the value of hard work; West Point had given me a calling. I didn't see the difference until it was almost too late. Mom worked as hard as she did out of necessity. She worked on a commission, selling bus tickets. No sales, no income.

But my work was not for a bus company; it was for the U.S. Army. "Duty, Honor, Country," the motto said. Pay strict attention to the mission, or a million ghosts in olive drab will haunt you. That's what MacArthur had told the Corps of Cadets, just a year after I graduated from West Point. MacArthur, Eisenhower, Patton, and all those before them, "the men of the Corps long dead." To them, we pledged our allegiance. To them we sang obeisance:

> The Corps, bareheaded, salute it,
>   With eyes up, thanking our God—
> That we of the Corps are treading
>   Where they of the Corps have trod—
> They are here in ghostly assemblage,
>   The men of the Corps long dead,
> And our hearts are standing attention
>   While we wait for their passing tread.

Ah yes, the men of the Corps long dead. Those men had, in a quiet, insidious way, established for me, and for thousands of others before and after me, the priorities by which we would live our lives, priorities that subordinated wife and children to the higher values. "If the Army wanted you to have a wife, they'd issue you one." Mission came first; everything else second. We never dreamed we had a choice.

Good soldiers, we bought the concept, every last one of us it seemed, everyone finally except the woman I married. It took her twelve years to act against the violation. Even the two "short tours" that put me first in Korea and then in Vietnam for twelve months, even those tours we took in stride. We had been called on to make the sacrifice. It was our duty. Two for the price of one was the unwritten contract that governed our lives. Eventually, women began to say no. Ann was one of the first.

When she realized that she could no longer subordinate herself to my job, it rocked me, undercutting the very principles upon which I had begun to live out my life. Instead of fighting like a man to hold on to those principles, I sat down for the first time in my life and thought about what it meant to be a father. I thought seriously about what *I* considered the highest values and began to wonder just exactly what it would take to hold my world together. Becoming a division commander seemed far less important than being a father. I had been around in my children's lives, but hadn't been immersed in them. I had a conviction that my business in life was business. If I worked hard enough and got promoted and brought home the bacon, everything else would follow. *Being there* turned out to be more complicated than I had imagined.

At Ann's insistence, I moved to an Army apartment for bachelor officers, a BOQ. There alone, trying to figure out how to respond to Ann's *crie de cour*—her urgent plea for space, I turned to down-and-out country music. Over on the other side of Lawton, Ann was playing Carly Simon and Carole King. In the BOQ room, I was listening to Willie Nelson. In the rhythm and whine of Nelson's plaint, I found my dad . . . for the first time. What grabbed me was not the sad story of rejection so often chronicled in the songs, but the spirit of soulful resignation and the latent optimism just beneath the surface. There was actually something mythic about what I was hearing. The ballads, the stories themselves, were as old as time. Nothing that was happening to me was so bad afterall. Others had had their props knocked out and survived to sing about it. I could too.

Through those songs, my own heart found its outlet, and in them I discovered solace and a father's independent spirit—a fierce and rugged individualism, a man not afraid to be fearful yet strong enough to survive. My world need not end.

Living apart from my children but near them in the same town, I got to know them better during the months of conflict and separation. When I went to them, I went with a purpose—usually to go fishing or to take them somewhere they wanted to go. I liked the fishing best because it gave us time to stand still and work together as we threaded the worms onto the hooks, bit the sinkers with our teeth, rigged the cane poles; it gave us time to wait on the banks of streams as we anticipated the thrill of the pull.

Whatever Patrick and Tim thought of those times they've never told me. For me the moments were special because they put me close to them and to my own dad. He had a reputation for being one of the best fishermen in a county full of sportsmen. The men and the women went together to the lakes and the rivers, and at the end of the long days in the sun, they got together to laugh and celebrate the day's catch. Pictures substantiate Dad's reputation—strings of fish, big ones . . . and always the smiling face, transformed by accomplishment. Standing on the creek bank together in Oklahoma, Patrick, Tim, and I gave each other lessons in fathering, and I began to sense for the first time in my life what I had actually missed. Climbing the corporate ladder had not given me such insight.

Many years later, after Ann and I had resolved the differences that were pushing us apart, after the children were grown, after I had found my dad in that Missouri cafe, I found him again, this time in the mountains of Wyoming. Nine of us had gone up to a lake near the end of an eight-day excursion on horseback. I had fishing on my mind before the trip and had asked for just one chance to catch a trout. I had had no experience fishing in mountain lakes, had never caught a trout. But I had heard stories, and somewhere deep in my bones I had a hankering to try it. Before the trip, a friend loaned me his spinning gear and a cloth pouch filled with lures and flies and other artificial whatnots.

Early that morning, we set out on horseback from the camp to go out of the valley into the mountains, up to Crater Lake. It was a long, winding climb, not nearly as steep as those on other days—no danger, nothing but the satisfaction of going up toward the sky, higher and higher until the view out into the Wind River Basin yanked our breath away. Near the top, we had to abandon our horses on a plateau and work our way on foot up the rock formations for one of the views, but our journey's end was higher yet, around the rocks and up so high we had to go down on foot across a small glacier field, and down even farther into the crater itself . . . to the lake. Only three of us wanted to fish.

I worked my way around the lake casting first one lure and then another without any luck until I found a place where I could leap out to a submerged boulder and cast into the middle of the lake. Standing apart pleased me; I could watch the others at the far end of the lake without being part of their noisiness. As I cast my line far out into the lake and let the lure go deep into the water before I began reeling, I sensed that I had found the perfect spot as well as the right technique. Casting, reeling, relaxing occasionally to let the lure drop down deeper before I tugged it, I had found a pleasing rhythm. The three trout I caught over the next few hours seemed something of a gift, and I was happy up there so high, out on the rock alone, to encounter my father's spirit.

He is not always easy to come across, but I've found him on other occasions in the books I read. There aren't many traces of him in my memory—we weren't together long enough and I know too few stories about him—so I have to depend on others to bring him to me. When they do, he tugs at me. Often it takes no more than an image to bring him to life. Sam Pickering, in "Son and Father," tells of walking into his father's room one evening finding him asleep, "pajamas . . . inside out, as mine invariably are." Sam saw on the bed an older version of himself, positions identical: "right leg pulled high toward the chest, and left thrust back and behind with the toes pointed, seemingly pushing us up and through the bed." During that moment of insight, "youth's false sense of superiority" fell away, and Sam realized something about likenesses and the absurdity of repudiation. Had my dad been standing near me on that boulder in Wyoming, watching me land the trout, he would have known by the rhythm of my casting and my lingering smile of satisfaction that we too are bound in strange ways. I no longer think of repudiation.

Carthage, Tennessee, tied Sam Pickering's father to a world of particulars and family values; it tied him to life. In turn he tied young Samuel to the same life. Looking back on their life together, Sam claims that "Pickerings lived quiet lives, cultivating their few acres and avoiding the larger world with its abstractions of honor, service, and patriotism. For them country meant the counties in which they lived, not the imperial nation. . . . With the exception of the Civil War, the struggles of the nation have not touched us." He finds strength in this response to life: "we are soft and, in our desires, subconscious or conscious, to remain free, have become evasive. Few things are simple though, and this very evasiveness may be a sign of a shrewd or even tough vitality"—or perhaps a sign of some great historical myth recreating itself in human terms.

Looking back on my youth, measuring it against the books I read now and the life I lived with my own sons, I yearn for only one thing my father might have given me. I grew up a child of the matriarchate, spending my life among the women. At the end of those hot, summer days, no matter what I had been doing, I returned to a house where there was no male influence. When I went away to college, I knew almost nothing about the way men and women act in the privacy of their own homes, and I knew precious little about the way grown men act in the company of other men, apart from the women. Going to West Point was a way into that world, but it was no substitute for the one I had been denied as I grew up. I sense that void in my life even today when I read about the loss in southern books, many of them written by men I have come to know and admire during these years of searching.

Roy Reed gave me a glimpse into that masculine life a few years ago when I was reading *Looking for Hogeye*. At the time, I was writing an essay of my own about mother-son journeys of separation. In the early drafts, I was overvaluing the matriarchate. Roy's essays caught me up short, put me back on track, led my imagination through the mother to the father, and let me see more clearly how the higher and the deeper values can manifest themselves in the lives of men. He also renewed my interest in tough-minded perseverance at a time when I was tiring of younger Army colleagues who still persisted in subordinating their lives to a calling they had not taken time to examine.

In "Spring Comes to Hogeye," it is not a woman who is close to nature but a man. Roy writes lovingly of Ira Solenberger whose life is so closely tied to the seasons that he, in concert with spring's late coming, knows intuitively to plant his crops late. Roy respects this old man's perception, cares about him. He makes us see that Ira dies in harmony with the seasons. His existence has followed a mysterious rhythm of ebb and flow. In a larger sense, Ira is important to Roy because his death signals the loss of a special breed of hill people. He relishes country folks' "plain damned meanness" and savors their sense of community; they "look after one another. . . . The trash take care of their own, not out of goodness but out of necessity. There is no one else to do it." Those hill folks know something important about community and survival, something distinctly masculine, and a touch mysterious.

In "Fall" Roy takes us into the woods with a "bunch" of hunters, some old, some young. We might just be in the Mississippi woods with Faulkner tracking bear, but this ritual develops on a smaller, more accessible, scale. The hunter's primary business is squirrel hunting. Roy's is the "exhilarating mystery that puzzles every hunter: the discovery that he can detect the presence of game by some sense that is beyond hearing, seeing or even smelling." Throughout this essay, Roy intersperses another narrative that begins in 1943 against the backdrop of war. It is a story about the "expectations that every Southern boy has a right to see filled at a certain time"—a narrative of male ritual: the first hunt, the first drink, the first kill. That ritual "tied the boy not only to the uncle but, more importantly, to his father, and tied the two of them to the ancestral woods." But then, "the son lost his taste for it." Hunting became a "single ritual hunt each year," and the government flooded the land. The "bond was dissolved and the son set adrift from his own blood." "Fall" is a story of cultural disintegration embedded in a story of perpetuation, of renewal and mystery. Like Ira Solenberger, Roy's hunting neighbors live close enough to the land to live the myth of community. In that myth we find the story of our survival.

Compare their view of the hunt to Allen Tate's: "One September day in the valley below Sewanee, twenty-five years ago, I shot a dove that fell into the weeds, and when I found her she was lying head up with a gout of blood in each eye. I shot her again. Her life had been given to my memory; and I have never hunted from that day." Tate explains his decision: "The feminine memory says: Here is that dying dove; you must really kill it this time or you will not remember it from all the other birds you have killed; take it or leave it; I have given it to you." One writer sees only the deeper values and not the highest. The other sees beyond the killing to the continuity, sees within the image of death itself the stuff of survival. My father, I suspect, was not much of a hunter, but he had access to that community of men; he had access to the story of perpetuation; he knew about the mystery of renewal. I know it too now, as a story, but he could have given it to me as a boy, firsthand, and I could have passed it on to my sons as experience. It is a loss I can only recover secondhand.

William Humphrey, whom I do not know, has given me the clearest insight into what my sons, my father, and I might have missed. Humphrey discovered the stuff of survival as a kid in Texas. In his memoir, *Farther Off from Heaven,* he resurrects a tough, wiry father every bit as wild as my own dad. He frames his memoir with his father's premature death. The fatal automobile wreck on the Fourth of July, 1937, was a strange, ironic emancipation for a boy of thirteen, but he survived because of a father's gift. Hunting was for the two of them an intimate, life-sustaining experience. The father himself had taken to the woods as a sanctuary from his tyrannical parents; he was, at first, the hunted. On his own in the woods, he learned to survive. He went there to verify the stories of danger told by outsiders; he went there "to see the dragons in their den." What he learned, he passed on to his son.

Reinventing years later the morning on which he and his mother accompanied his father's mangled body in the ambulance ride to Paris, Texas, Humphrey thought of the magic of those woods he shared with his father. He remembered the break of day, the pristine moment of first light, remembered that the "change seemed chemical, like a photographic print in the developer in the dimness of the darkroom, the image appearing out of nothingness, then rapidly becoming distinct, recognizable, familiar." He remembered his father's transformation in the woods, that "old boyish wonder": "My oneness with him gave me some of his sense of oneness with that world." That world—their world, the world of the father and the son—was a world of trust and companionship, a world in which the two were on such intimate terms they could dispense with talk. Deep in the woods on an alligator hunt, Humphrey claims to have found "along with the deepening strangeness . . . a familiarity, as though one had been here before, but in another life"; he expected around one of the turns that the "long-forgotten, universal mother tongue" would come back to them; he thought they might very well reenter paradise. Telling this story, Humphrey reenacts Marlow's journey up the river to visit Kurtz, but these voyagers come back bound together for life. No need for Marlow's noble lie. They do not submit. They meet the alligator-dragon, subdue it, make it their own. They return, young and renewed.

Death, then, was not a new experience for the thirteen-year-old boy, but the sudden, revolting loss of a father was. Premature death shocked him because it left him alone. We can judge the severity of the jolt and the power of his father's influence by Humphrey's reaction on the night before the funeral: "My last night's sleep in Clarksville, with my father's body lying in the next room, would be my last ever, I vowed. No visits home for me, no reopening of wounds. It was a vow I was to keep for thirty-two years."

But finally, like a salmon's, Humphrey's "homing instincts" got the best of him, and he defied his vows; he too discovered the folly of repudiation. Back in town with a guide, he comes upon two boys playing in the cemetery; they offer to help him find the grave they think he's searching for: "Looking at either of them was like looking at myself through the wrong end of binoculars. I gave them half a dollar apiece, a token repayment for all the many nickels that men of Clarksville had given me in my time . . . thanked them; said no, we were not looking for any grave, what we were looking for was just the opposite: some spot where there was not any grave, where there was still room for one. Why? Was somebody dead? No; not yet."

The Texas Humphrey had come back to was changed, just as Carthage, Hogeye, and Hamburg have changed. Lytle was dead right about the onslaught of industrialism. But something remains of place that is as timeless as those riverbottoms Humphrey entered with his father, something deep. It calls us back wherever we are, calls us back into community. Whether our fathers were there or not, whether they took us literally on the hunt, whether they left us land or left us landless, there hovers about the place a presiding spirit, masculine, indomitable, inviolable.

There is mystery. My father, I used to think, simply was not there. I have discovered over time, that he was, still is. He's there, like the place; he's in my bones. I know it by the fives I make. I know it by the cars I drive and the way I drive them, know it too by the smiling way I ask for recognition and confirmation. I know it too by what I learned from my own sons, standing and fishing together on the banks of those streams in Oklahoma. But I know it especially by my evolving relationship with the woman in my head. Like my father, I know her power, know how easy it is to turn my life over to anima, seductress that she is, dancing there with her little cowboy in the starlight cafe. But I know too what he never seemed to learn. I know that she will not always stand up in the light of day, will not always stand up to the higher values. The real woman, outside my head, might, but the one inside is a different matter. She can lead me to destruction or she can save me. Her duality is tricky business.

I have discovered that anima has a partner. Anima—soul,

imagination, the woman in my head who is not a mere woman—anima and animus have been there all along in my psyche: a divine pair, a syzygy. James Hillman suggests that to "imagine in pairs and couples is to think mythologically. Mythical thinking connects pairs into tandems rather than separating them into opposites." In my own acts of imagining, I recognize animus—a shaping, criticizing spirit. It has given me what Hillman calls "distance from mood." Perhaps it has given me what Sam Pickering might call the "right distance." I see more clearly now how the syzygy manifests itself in our time, how we can have "shrewd, tough vitality" on the home front, how the farmer can live in nature, how the intimacy of the hunt can match the intimacy of a good marriage. I see again how toughness can be a virtue. What I find in my own imagination is a happy marriage of the highest and the deepest values, a mounting respect for the preservation of the community through close living, living so close to earth that we do not lose touch of it. I see there the myth of our time. And I hear from the bottom land of my imagination the deep cry of ancestral voices.

Imagining Lives of Our Own

In psychic life, it is the heat, the fire of passion, the flame and ardor of emotion that provide the basis of illumination.
ERICH NEUMANN

IN MY EARLY FORTIES I was seized occasionally by a compelling urge to escape—not to run away from it all but to escape once in awhile, responsibly. The sleek, bright orange MG that I bought to wind round and round the roads outside the back gate of the Army post took me nowhere, but I got there fast. I also bought the Klipsch speakers I'd been wanting since high school, bought them so I could hear Beethoven's "Hymn to Joy" as if I were inside Beethoven's own head. I wanted to be transformed.

I'd been inside Willie Nelson's head, or he in mine, for a long time. "Black Rose" was no surprise to me. I understood how a "cain-raising man" could turn from woman to woman for salvation and be left with nothing more to claim time after time than "a Rose of a different name"—a man duped by a mere projection, the woman inside his head wreaking havoc, transfiguring the ones outside.

Whether the woman in my head was there to hold me in tormenting limbo or show me the way, I didn't know. Even C. G. Jung saw her in one guise as nixie, siren, lamia, succubus—the mad woman of fairy tale "who infatuates young men and sucks the life out of them." But Jung would also see her as a way into the life behind consciousness, as anima, the feminine aspect of the male, his guide. Somehow, I had to come to terms with her.

I REALLY COULDN'T BELIEVE it was happening as I drove out the back gate of the Military Academy, my mind guiding me down the river of my soul's desire. But before I knew it, as I crossed Freedom Bridge, I started peeling off my clothes: sweater first, followed by the tie, followed by the epaulets. Out the window they went, all the military ornaments, the badges of my profession. Then came the shoes, one at a time so I could still operate the pedals, then the trousers one leg at a time. Rid of the black stripes, the last vestiges of the disciplined world I was leaving behind, I struggled into my jeans and relaxed. Nobody could see me. Behind my Vuarnets, I was invisible. "Scarlet Fever," blaring on the stereo, might have turned me around had I stopped to think, but I was beside myself, hell-bent. Scarlet, in one of her many guises, had become "the envy of my dreams."

She was waiting there where she said she'd be, high atop the meadow, and as I made my way up to her side, I wondered about the lay of the land—where we might go, what we might say. When I reached her side, I looked momentarily beyond her, into the distance where I could see for miles down the valley, and then our eyes met, hers reflecting the hues of the flowers rising from her breast, yellow daffodils and a single red crocus flaming up. Her radiant face, bathed in colored light, was surrounded by vine leaves flowing out of her embroidered shift. The leaves ran up her neck through the flowers and around her head, haloing her beauty. As I reached out to touch her, she moved comfortably into the space I created for her, and we sank to the ground entwined, awash at once in the rhythms of time, lost.

Maybe it was the sound of a mowing machine on the path behind us, perhaps just a call back from my conscious mind, but as the spell was broken and I discovered my hands, I spoke, I thought, as if for the first time: "Tha's got the nicest arse of anybody. It's the nicest, nicest woman's arse as is! An' ivry bit of it is a woman. . . . It's a bottom as could hold the world up, it is."

"Sir . . . Colonel Hoy, sir, you're not listening again. Come on sir, pay attention. I need to talk to you."

I heard her voice but resisted. I had been staring into the sunlight so long I didn't want to come back. But she was calling out of some deep need. So I swung my chair around, turning away from the window to face her and was shocked to see how beautiful she was standing there with the lambent sunlight playing over her body. She looked for all the world like a seraph caged in bars of light, flushed, burning feverishly. I could feel her passion.

"Sir, he sat there by me last night at the banquet, and he knew. 'Miss Goodman,' he said, 'I understand that you missed the picture-taking formation this afternoon.' Measured, deliberate, you know how he talks, sir. He went on baiting me. Wanted to know why I wouldn't pose together with the other women for a class picture, without the men, for *Life*. He couldn't understand the irony. Can you believe the Superintendent did that to me at a formal dining-in? I was his dinner partner, and he ruined it."

"Molly, that was almost twenty-four hours ago. What's going on? Why are you still so riled up?" I didn't expect an answer. She was mad, frustrated, more agitated than I had ever seen her. Couldn't seem to stand still. And I sensed a problem larger than the missed formation.

"Maybe," I suggested, "the Supe was expressing his own limitation. He's bound, limited, like the rest of us. But you did ignore an order and stand apart from the group of women who helped you survive this place. . . . Why don't you sit down and stay awhile. Do you have a parade?"

"No sir. The other regiments have a parade. I can talk for a while, but we'll have to listen for them to march back in the area. I can't be late for supper formation."

I wanted to ask her if she had talked to her tactical officer about missing the formation. He should have understood her conflict, but I suspected that he wouldn't see her side very clearly. I was right.

"I've already talked to my tac. He said I had no right to miss a required formation, but I have to call him back later to see what will happen."

"Okay, Molly, let's pull back a little and think. Imagine what must have gone through the Supe's head when someone told him you wouldn't pose for the picture. *They broke down the doors of this male bastion, earned their spurs, overcame our prohibitions, survived, and now they can't even get together for a picture.* From his point of view, women have gotten everything they wanted. You defy his logic, you know."

She was listening, settling down a bit, but I knew I was caught in the middle again—torn between my desire to change things and my anger at people who wouldn't think independently without worrying about the "duty concept." The Commandant called always for a "stiffening of the vertebrae." He insisted on letter-of-the-law obedience. I never heard anyone from on high call for a supple mind. We were, nevertheless, supposed to be educating young men and women for a lifetime of service. Who would serve more wisely, I wondered, the obedient servant or the maverick?

"Molly, do you really expect the Supe to understand how that formation—the one he approved after careful deliberation—singles you women out, separates all of you from the very men you've been trying to join? Wouldn't he expect pride to draw you into the picture, into a moment of public celebration. It probably wouldn't occur to him that celebration for a woman could be intensely private, that you don't need public confirmation. He can't get inside your imagination."

"Well, they never can."

"Really. Who are they? Right now, you're having trouble getting inside his head. We've all got our notion of how things ought to be. Why, for God's sake, after four years of this stuff does his problem bother you so much?"

She got up again and walked over to the bookshelves, obviously tired of my efforts to reconcile her. I didn't like my little speeches either because they put me too much at odds with her. But I was growing weary of the women's whining, weary of their claims to independence and their calls for reassurance. I wanted them to act like men, wanted them to walk on their own two feet without my counsel or anyone else's. But I wanted them the other way too.

They had come to us alone, and we kept them apart from each other except in their rooms. Two here, three there—integrated in the barracks with the men. Yet separate and unequal. The male world they entered afforded no support. These women were first and always would be. The Army they were about to enter would adjust reluctantly. So would they, again and again.

One of Molly's bitingly sarcastic stories had come to me signed "The fourth male personality of Molly Goodman." Gender switching was normal for them, but seldom deliberate. The first stressful year stopped their periods. Few in the chain-of-command noticed: the doctors on sick call, later the medical staff, finally a major in the psychology department recording facts for posterity—a handful of observers, mostly male. Those of us charged with teaching and development didn't know. Split, we split them... deeply, I think.

The institution hadn't learned to deal openly, publicly with women's bodies. We talked about "physiological differences"; that was our corporate phrase. Those differences would keep women from doing as many push-ups and pull-ups as men, something to do with muscle mass and bone structure. We said nothing about that other bloody business, nothing about normal, healthy differences. No one had anything to say about psychic changes, about moods, about the real significance of a woman's body shutting down, denying its own natural rhythms. We had stopped their periods but had no idea what was growing inside their psyches. Physiological differences would keep women from being all they ought to be. For most men, that was the crucial fact.

For women, the problem was more complicated. They were in a male institution, seeking acceptance, seeking equal treatment. They were at West Point because they wanted to be. Something inside their heads was urging them, pushing them into it, demanding that they do it, some spirit of independence, some inner necessity. The rules of the game and the nature of the commitment seemed to demand it. Those young women had sought equality without realizing for a moment how such a notion could turn into its opposite.

I learned about the periods from Molly, three years after her freshman year when stress, loss of body fat, and who knows what else, had changed their private lives. But we changed their public lives in more serious and subtle ways, depriving them of their right to be women. They were issued skirts, but rarely wore them. Male pressure forbade it. The idea was to blend in: short hair, no earrings, gray flattening shirts, gray pants with black stripes, the standard belt with brass buckle, shiny low quarters, black socks—clothes without shape. Eventually, the women would wear tiny gold-post earrings, but they would also have to wear men's ties with their class shirts. Nevertheless, they prevailed, and after plebe year they began to redress some of the imbalances.

One night when I was serving as academic officer-in-charge, going around the barracks to observe study conditions, I found women in the hallways and in their rooms who had transformed themselves after the evening meal. They had rid themselves of the shapeless clothes, washed their hair, and donned T-shirts with their fatigue trousers. Moving about the barracks, they had little in common with the female cadets who sat in my classes during the day. They had reclaimed their bodies.

Even during the day at formations, they added a new dimension to hazing, standing there nose-to-nose, chest-to-chest, close, eyeball-to-eyeball with an unsuspecting plebe, testing him while testing the limits of their own sexuality. They might look like a man in a class uniform, but they smelled better. If they knew what they were doing, the plebe was never sure. Neither were their own classmates at company parties. In civilian clothes, dressed to the nines, they were more difficult to think of as men. No one could get it quite right—who they were, why they were there, where they were going.

When I met Molly in one of my literature classes during her senior year, she was still curious enough about what had happened to her over those years to want to write about it. Swinging back and forth between her personalities, she tested me, found me receptive, equally curious, and safe. I could talk openly to her about herself. That I was a man made the talk more interesting. She was, after all, trying to reclaim her femininity, and I, paused at the menopausal node of my life, enjoyed the intimacy of a young woman. I was intrigued too by anima, my feminine aspect: feeling, intuition, imagination . . . my soul. Molly—my own private response to Molly—could tell me much about myself. But close to her there in the room, it was difficult to decide whether she was Rose in another guise or a seraph bringing light.

During those years, I thought often of gender differences. "Ought not education to bring out and fortify the differences rather than the similarities?" Virginia Woolf had asked half a century earlier. But at West Point, we were bent on sameness. The defiant male chorus demanded it, mocking the women when they fell short on push-ups, or when they failed in some way to measure up to the old dispensations. Yet Molly Goodbody wouldn't be mocked. She wouldn't give in.

Her back was still to me as the late afternoon sun, streaming through the windows, illuminated her. We had not worked our way to the source of her frustration. So I reached back to adjust the blind. I wanted to take off the bars, uncage her if I could.

"Molly, what about your paper? You making any progress?"

"Well, sir, not as much as you expect, but I've narrowed the topic a bit. I've been thinking about doing something called 'Floors, Doors, and Ceilings: An Examination of Sexual Spaces from Salinger to Hawkes.'" She paused long enough to smirk and then continued playfully. "But you'll probably crucify me if I go off on another flight of fancy. So I'll probably stick with Lady Chatterley and try to figure out what Lawrence is talking about."

She had already written about Mailer's *American Dream,* trying to find out what Mailer knew about women and about men and women together. Now, she was turning back in time to Lawrence.

"I'm not sure if Mellors has any more balls than Clifford," she continued, agitated again. "They're all suffering from sex in the head. Lawrence too. What's that tripe at the end about the crocus and 'the little pentecost flame?'"

She didn't wait for answers, didn't really want any. She was devouring Lawrence's words and mine, spitting them back up. Her mind was ablaze. She wanted to know what Lawrence meant by a "warmhearted fucking." I wanted to tell her that the metaphor pointed to something so sacred that talk was a violation. But that wouldn't satisfy her and might push her toward a kind of literalness that neither of us could afford. Talk, Lawrence knew, had obscured life's most accessible mystery. "Warmhearted fucking" had been taken by a whole generation as a mere physical feat. The myth in our time had lost its savor; the metaphor had become a fact. Talking to Molly about the metaphor itself posed no problem. But passing over into talk of my own experience was another matter, a violation of my obligation.

And worse, she might not want it. It might undo the image she had of me—that I had fostered or that she had elicited to match some image she had in her head. I had to get to the mystery by a safer route.

"Molly, have you read William Irwin Thompson yet?"

"No sir, I haven't. I had to take the obstacle course this morning, and yesterday and the day before I had staff problems to solve, and the night before we had seminars. I really haven't had time. I'm sorry, sir. I'm gonna spend the weekend working on my paper."

"Okay. Try to get to Thompson; he might take you outside the limits of your own experience. He's good on the relationship between the higher consciousness of language and the lower consciousness of sexuality. Think about that as you think about Connie, Mellors, and all that early talk in the novel about sex in the head. Think about *submission* too. Try to understand Lawrence's suggestion. A woman friend of mine would probably tell you that Lawrence 'doesn't mean yielding to tyranny but giving in to respect.' She would be very close, I think. That's hard for us to understand these days, but it's a fairly simple notion if you can set aside momentarily much of what you've learned and ease yourself away from the implied threat. See if you can enter the novel unencumbered, free of your cultural baggage. . . . Tough as it is, that's your imaginative task."

"What's a man supposed to do in this bargain?" she fired back. "Take his clue from Mailer and give her the time of her time as he strips away the layers one by one until the two of them lie there together in the spasms of the great mystery—he the agent of her salvation?"

"Not exactly. But in a way Lawrence and Mailer aren't far apart. Violence plays a larger part in Mailer's metaphor, though. The male warrior performs heroic feats for himself and the woman. Mailer's man, trying to find himself, can't always get it up."

"You're right about that."

"Well, at least you haven't lost your sense of humor. Not a bad sign on a bad day. Anyway, Mailer's hero is always thinking about what he's doing; he's often outside the experience, acting out his self-appointed role as agent of salvation. Lawrence preaches *tenderness* in lieu of tyranny. Submission for women, tenderness for men, the two imponderables. Lawrence, like Mailer, hangs on to male authority, but for him there's an equal authority for the woman. He calls it 'hensureness.' And the male's 'cocksureness' has little to do with bullying."

She seemed to reach for the sky, joining her palms over her head for a moment. I wondered if she had caught something in the cupped space between her hands. As she folded her arms across her chest, she began to speak in another voice.

"You know, I think bullying is the problem. That's why I can't quite find my way in this organization, even now. I still don't know whether I can make it to graduation. Last night, after the banquet, I had a very strange, weird experience."

She had been leaning against the filing cabinet, but suddenly moved away, set in motion again by the story she was about to tell. I caught a whiff of her perfume as she rustled over into the sunlight. Her blue eyes stopped dancing.

"There I was in my room and everything was laid out for today, the uniform and the boots and all that stuff, and I had this vision of myself at Fort Bragg in battle fatigues with jump wings on. I was scared. My body didn't seem to belong in the uniform ... didn't belong in that place, didn't seem to belong to me, you know what I mean? I couldn't imagine myself jumping from airplanes, playing those roles, being there."

Her face lost its tautness as her voice lost its edge. She moved over to the chair closest to my desk, hesitated for a moment, settled lightly into it, and turned her shining eyes upon me.

"At moments like that I don't know what to do, sir."

The "sir" was her last line of defense—her way of warding me off as she got closer. Her sir for my eagles. Fair play.

"I've come so far . . . too far I think, to throw it all away. What am I supposed to do?"

"Molly, we've been over this a thousand times. You know that. Other things have upset you, not this much, but you've been here before, out of sorts with your antagonists. I really don't think you can hope for radical change. I've been underground in this world for a long time, and I still like what I'm doing. I don't want people like you to bail out and leave it to the diehards. We need responsible mavericks, people who care enough to question."

I had often grown tired of fighting for change, but not tired enough to turn it over to people who were serving time so they could move up the corporate ladder. I liked being a safe distance from the institution I was serving, enjoyed resisting the romantic fictions many other men believed in. I thought about Santayana's claim that "masks are arrested expressions and admirable echoes of feeling, at once faithful, discreet, and superlative." He believed that we "define our sovereign temper" by the "visage we assume," that one's "deliberate character is more truly oneself than is the flux of our involuntary dreams." I wasn't so sure, wasn't at all ready to "crystallize [my] soul into an idea," but Santayana had a point about social discipline.

"Molly, you might try one other thing. Think of Bragg as a fictive world, one you can enter at will. The trick, of course, will be to move in and out of that world deliberately, by an act of intellection. You need to be in charge of the switching, or at least be aware of when you've switched. There will be plenty for you to do at Bragg. No need to lose your soul to the corporation. You've got spunk and conviction. They'll get used to you. It won't be easy, but they'll do it. Your work will win out in the end."

She had come momentarily to rest. Outside, the cannon broke the silence. Soon there would be another formation for the evening meal and then a bugle call for evening study period. The obligations would go on and on.

"Sir, can I come over again this weekend and bring Jim and my poems? They're getting better."

"I'm sure they are. But before you come over, think about staying around for graduation. What the hell, you've still got at least a month to make up your mind. . . . Then again, you could go ahead and resign. I'm sure the Supe would waive your military obligation, wouldn't you think?"

She smiled. Anger and frustration hadn't diminished her spirit.

"I hear the sounds of agony outside," I said. "They're coming back from the public performance. All shine and precision. Happy band of brothers they, marching home together. I guess we need to move on too. I have some reading to do for tomorrow's classes. You know my advice about West Point anyway."

"Yeah, yeah, I know, sir. 'Make up your mind what you want to be Goodman and then get on with it. And Goodman, if you decide to leave, don't let the doorknob hit you in the ass.' Right, sir?"

"Right Molly." And she disappeared behind the swinging door, smiling again, back over her shoulder. Watching her, I heard Mellor's words playing again inside my head: "Tha's got the nicest arse of anybody. It's the nicest, nicest woman's arse as is!"

I knew that I had been wrestling with my soul. Through Molly I had begun to understand James Hillman's claim about the necessary marriage between Eros and Psyche, his claim that "creative insights come at the raw and tender edge of confrontation, at the borderlines where we are most sensitive and exposed—and, curiously, most alone." To meet Psyche, to find my soul, I had to become Eros, answering Psyche's call for involvement, else I was destined to remain at the edge of life, apart from it, a mere spectator.

MOLLY GRADUATED and rushed headlong into an Army that was unprepared for her and the others. The summer following their graduation, I was invited to dinner with five of them at Fort Sill, Oklahoma, where I had been sent to teach senior officers and high-ranking civilians to write more effectively. Once during the meal, the women seemed to forget that I was with them. Their talk turned to careers and babies, how they might handle the two together. They joked about what it might be like. "Hey, Herbie, your mom wears combat boots. Ninnie, ninnie, ninnie." But they planned anyway.

By the time I saw those women in Oklahoma, some of their classmates were already married to other classmates, headed for what the Army would later call "joint domicile" assignments. Husbands and wives would be stationed within a hundred miles of each other in Germany, in Korea, in the states. Wherever. Guaranteed.

Before the summer was over, some of the women would have their assignments changed within the field artillery because the Army had decided—on second thought—that it would be unwise and inappropriate to assign them to certain combat-ready units such as the 82d Airborne Division. They remained separate and unequal, and it still didn't sit well. Molly did not go to Fort Bragg. Instead, she went to Europe where she eventually commanded a combat-ready Lance missile unit. The difference between Europe and Bragg was a matter of degree and prestige; it was also a matter of gender.

Over the years at West Point, my wife and I kept sponsoring a few students of our own choosing, providing an occasional meal or weekend haven for those needing a room for parents or space of their own to sort out problems. Eventually, I found myself greeting old friends at receptions during parent weekends and graduation ceremonies. The computer occasionally outdid itself and matched me in class with the son or daughter of old acquaintances from Arkansas or from the Army, folks I hadn't seen for years. These chance encounters always reminded me of the passing years. No longer could I stand around at receptions joking with male colleagues about the mothers, trying to see who among us could eye the good-looking one who had had the boy early and stayed stunning. Suddenly—it certainly seemed sudden—the mothers were younger, and I was looking at them from a new vantage post. And of course there were the daughters, Molly and her avatars. And the women officers on the faculty.

One afternoon when I returned to my office after classes and committee meetings, I had a letter from Molly. She had been invited by the English department to attend graduate school in preparation for an assignment to the West Point faculty. Her letter, the first I had received from her since the summer of her graduation, was a request for a recommendation. I had known about her selection and was pleased that she, along with others from her class, would be joining the faculty for a three-year assignment. They would be among the first women graduates to come back. But by the time they finished their graduate work, I would be retired, missing them altogether. It was my one regret about leaving because I wanted to see what they would bring to the classroom, what lessons they had learned that would make them effective teachers and counselors for the men and women they would get to know during those three years. Other students of mine had returned already, officers I had taught during my first assignment to the department. But I wanted to see what the women would do, how they might bring change and new insights . . . and I would miss it.

I had kept up with Molly and three other students who were in the first literature class I had taught after joining the tenured faculty. Two men were out of the Army, one a technical writer, the other a law student. Two women were still in; both had commanded units; both were on the way to graduate school; both would teach English. I had thought of them often over the years as I prepared my classes, thought about their spirited reactions and their needs. They asked more of me than any class I've ever taught, but they helped me find my way back into the classroom and gave me a clear sense of what I ought to try to do for my students.

During the ten years that had passed since their graduation, the women in my classes had taught me more than the men; they had kept me looking for new ways to interpret texts, pushing me as Molly had. With the men, I enjoyed an easy, playful camaraderie. When we read a story like "Araby," I had no trouble getting them to understand the young narrator's obsession with Mangan's sister. They responded readily to the "soft rope of her hair" and her "brown figure" and knew instantly what the young narrator means when he tells us that his "body was like a harp and her words and gestures were like fingers running upon the wires." But the women in class wouldn't give us the pleasure of an unexamined, male reaction to the text. They saw clearly that Mangan's sister is an object of desire for the young narrator, and they often hooted at the men for not understanding how they project their own desires onto women.

Neither group had an easy time with the spiritual implications of those projections. The men and the women had trouble coming to terms with the narrator's "confused adoration," "the gauntlet" he was running, and the "chalice" he sought, and the hooting women often forgot their own susceptibility to adoration. Everyone resented the ending when Joyce turns the lights out on the boy's fair, there in the very church that is Araby. We all expect the lights of desire to burn forever, unextinguished, and knowledge of the young narrator's "fib" amounted to self-knowledge about our own deceptions.

Those discussions always sent me back into my head, back into my imagination to examine my own life. I had begun to see myself as a happy victim, unable to deny my basic male urge, destined always to strive in some way to climb mountains and stake out new, conquerable territory. The terms of the metaphors changed, but the striving never let up. I found something both comforting and absurd about the feats I laid out for myself. The stories inside my head, the ones I concocted in order to live, began to seem more and more mythic, more and more commonplace. At bottom, they were the same stories we read and discussed every day in the classroom.

I took immodest comfort knowing that in many ways I had surpassed Virginia Woolf's archetypal patriarch, Mr. Ramsay. I was not, as Woolf claimed Ramsay was, stuck at R, unable to evolve. I was growing accustomed to the women in my life, those in my head and the ones I encountered from day to day, and if occasionally I had to pay homage to the beauty of the earth as Mr. Ramsay finally did at Woolf's behest, I accepted my fate charitably and more knowingly.

But John Updike's heroes, like James Joyce's, occasionally caught me up short. Still susceptible to wife-wooing and the seduction of language, I took great delight in Richard Maples, one of Updike's luckless heroes. Richard the modern-day hunter, reduced to wrestling meat "warm from the raw hands of the hamburger girl in the diner a mile away" comes home a mere errand boy. Wife and children form a crescent around the fire, eat their meals oblivious to Richard's thoughts about just rewards and the "parallel whiteness" of his wife's thighs exposed to the fire. Drunk on desire, Richard conjures Joyce from "a deep Dublin den." Seductive sounds. "Smacked smackwarm on her smackable warm woman's thigh. . . . Seven years since I wed wide warm woman, white-thighed. Wooed and wed. Wife." She hears nothing. All in Richard's head. Later, tired, in bed, reading, she falls asleep over Nixon and Alger Hiss. Betrayed, Richard skulks in the dark, lost in anger and desire and rejection. The women in class always liked this story; the men joined me in self-defense as we toyed with plausible cover-ups about effort and reward.

I liked to get them all going about *Sir Gawain and the Green Knight*. They always seemed to want to read the poem literally. Never could understand, without coaxing, that Gawain might have been traveling across psychic terrain as he made his way to the Green Giant's castle, that the lady who came to his chamber was as much a part of his psyche as say Molly's independence had been a part of hers. They had trouble with the medieval fair: the castle and the hunt and the green girdle, the fair of discovery, of temptation, of seduction, of honor, and of trespassing. It was fun to try to get them to see that the girdle was not a badge of shame; it was a confirmation of Gawain's humanity, a reminder of his complex personality. The woman was there to tempt him, to temper his idealistic heroism, to bring him down to the level of his own humanity. Perhaps she had been there in his head all along waiting for him to discover her.

My reading of *Gawain* put them at odds with their preconceived notions about themselves, made them think about the morality of betrayal, the benefits of failure, the transforming, healing significance of imagination. The poem gave them a new way to think of their relationships with each other. I always thought of Molly.

Her letter had put me in a good mood that day, and when

Nan Jo Hoy and Patrick Cleburn Hoy, 1933

Pat and his father, 1942

Pat showing Williard's picture to Scott, 1945

Pat in his senior year at West Point, 1961

Pat, Tim, Ann, and Patrick Hoy at Harvard, 1988

Ann called asking what time I'd be home, I was pleased that her day of teaching had gone well. She was ready to turn her positive energy toward projects at home, and I could sense where my evening would be spent even before I knew exactly what she had on her mind. I told her that I had gotten a letter from Molly.

"What does she need?" Ann asked.

I explained that Molly would be coming back from Germany and needed a letter for graduate school. Ann knew that we would be gone before Molly and others from her class returned from school, and she too was sorry. But we had to move on with our lives, and at that moment Ann had other things on her mind. "I was wondering if you'd frame *Theseus* tonight?"

She had wanted me to frame the print for a long time, but I had kept dragging my feet. It looked fine to me laminated, without a frame, but she kept insisting. When asked why, she just smiled.

I LIKED THESEUS UNFRAMED, standing there dominating the foreground, even dominating the minotaur. He seems to be musing about where to go, how to get out of the labyrinth the artist so cleverly raises in relief from the ground of the painting, giving the myth just the right emphasis. She locks Theseus dead center in that maze. And so he stands there caged, awaiting an answer, thinking perhaps that it will come from some secret messenger.

Theseus seems to have forgotten momentarily that he has a way out of the maze. Ariadne has already saved him, if only he could remember, if only he could remember to follow the thread of his own imagination. She would set him free.

"Why don't we talk about Theseus when I get home, Ann. I was thinking about working on tomorrow's lecture, but I could be talked into something else if you feel like fooling around a little bit."

"Why don't we go for a ride? See you later."

As I rode down the elevator, I settled against the brass rail, exhausted and happy. Teaching had become more and more satisfying over the years. I liked being tempted and tempered as students pushed me to find new explanations, new possibilities. I delighted in trying to prepare them to be good Army officers, but I liked most the way they made me confront my own foibles and inconsistencies, the way they made me face myself to find answers for them. They kept my imagination working at a fever pitch.

I left the elevator on the F-level, deep down in the building, and walked out into the fading afternoon light. The breeze off the river stirred my spirit as I sank into the MG and headed for home, shooting up the hill, through the tunnel, out into the open air. For a moment, just for a fleeting moment, I imagined myself transfigured, soaring free.

I thought again of Molly and the others, wondering whether they would have to wait, as I had, another fifteen or twenty years, for such moments of their own.

Conversing with Images

> *My effort to understand is a perpetual circling around
> a few obsessive images.*
> CHARLES SIMIC

> *We do well to read our lives with the same intensity we develop
> from learning to read our texts.*
> ROBERT SCHOLES

> *A vein of poetry exists in the hearts of all men.*
> THOMAS CARLYLE

I AM AT THE HELM of a forty-five-foot sailboat in the waters surrounding the British Virgin Islands. I have spent most of the morning at the helm, on a deck bench, on my back, looking up at the sails, looking occasionally across the bow to make sure no other boat is in my path. My sailing method seems to suit the man in charge. I have chosen a general direction—toward a destination—but my aim is not to get there by the most direct route; it is, as Annie Dillard might say, to sail on solar wind. So I am on my back, looking up at the jib, determined to sail the wind as fast as I can for the sheer pleasure of it.

I have a good feel for the wind, something my son taught me. Watching him sail my small catboat on the Hudson River and at Cape Cod, I learned to relax, to sail by the seat of my pants . . . or to continue the metaphor, by the feel of the wind on my face. Here in the Caribbean, I feel the wind on my face, sense her power and her direction; on the bench, on my back, I also feel the wind and the sea come together. The boat finds its fit, and I feel tautness at the helm, the lift, an exhilirating shift in the speed of the boat. As I sail, I feel the sea pull and haul on the boat, her gentle corkscrewing power moving us roundabout. But I relax into the mystery of it all, knowing without a shadow of a doubt that we are moving forward while going roundabout. The sea and the wind and I will get us to our destination. I need only remain attentive to the forces playing on my spirit.

In my head, I am seized by something almost as lovely as the rush of love. A cacophony of voices chatter to me out of the depths of memory, and I want to tell my fellow sailors what I hear—want to tell them why I feel so good riding on the sea's power and feel so ill at ease in her depths, want to talk about Conrad and the "destructive element," want to explore the way other people's books and ideas limit and entangle my own sexual metaphor of the sea, want to come to terms with that childhood experience when my dad jokingly threatened to cut me up for fish bait and throw me in the water, scaring me half out of my wits, want to talk about William Carlos Williams's "Death is not the end of it"—but I can say little. Amidst all the memories, Bob Scholes speaks loudest, and I hear him reminding me that moments such as this "must be seized." "When digested," he had claimed, "they become the very body of our consciousness, as the food we eat becomes our flesh." I want to talk, want to tell my secrets, but I don't know how to tell my story yet. Besides, my friends on board aren't with me. My experiences at the moment are not theirs. Yet they sense that I'm in a crazy, exuberant mood; they seem to know that I'm out of joint with time.

"Are you keeping a journal of our little voyage?" Margarita asks after an hour or so of sailing.

"I'm trying to keep up with how all this feels," I tell her.

"Does anyone get to read it?"

"No, I don't think so."

CONVERSING WITH IMAGES

I would like to explain to her that I don't yet have the language to talk about how it feels, that eventually I hope to think my way through those feelings and sort out the voices. But it's too early to say anything coherent, so I babble about something *primordial*. The others like the word.

During the next four or five days of sailing, Bob Scholes keeps playing in my imagination. He had set my mind and my friends' minds whirling almost six months earlier at a conference in Seattle, and we had spent the better part of an afternoon talking about what he had told us.

As the foundation for a talk about reading and writing, Scholes had chosen three images—a painting (*The Education of the Virgin*), a personal experience on a small sailboat, and a photograph (*Tomoko in the Bath*). What unified his talk, what made those three images so powerful, was the way he illuminated them, the way he read the images against his own life to show us what they said to each other and to us about mothering and love and human development. Nowhere was his point more clear than in his account of the boat trip he and his wife had taken down the Sakonnet River toward Rhode Island Sound. "What had happened was a simple thing, really," he says. We began "to encounter the great ground swells that come from far out in the ocean and rise higher as the bottom underneath them begins to affect their progress. These swells were gentle but immensely powerful, and they raised and lowered our little boat with awesome ease. This was a rhythm," he goes on to say, a rhythm that "whispered of primal things and we understood what it was saying. It was like returning to a state before birth and listening to your mother's heart beat, pumping life into your own arteries as well, for it spoke of life and death and said that they were one." Or, at least, that's what the rhythm said to Bob Scholes, and presumably had said earlier to Buck Mulligan ("She is our great sweet mother") and even earlier to Swinburne.

INSTINCT FOR SURVIVAL

The sea, or Scholes's experience of the sea that day as he came out of the Sakonnet River, spoke to him of the Great Mother; it reminded him of primal origins; it also reminded him of the end of things and their beginning, his life, his death; it reminded him too of God and of the mystery of creation. But he didn't say much about either. Busy creating the story of his own life, Scholes left out the story about the unspoken language that had connected the three images in the first place and that's what I, as a writer, wanted to hear more about. When all of us who had been so moved by his talk stopped chattering, I yearned for a great deal more on that balmy afternoon in Seattle.

Gripped by Scholes's images, I went back to my hotel room to be alone, and I began to write, began to recreate a part of my own life. Scholes's three images had become mine even as he talked about them, and I wanted to see how they would work on me. Writing, I began to understand something I had never known. I began to see that deep in my imagination, images have a language of their own . . . a prelingual language that I can understand, if only I have the patience to listen. That language, the compelling unspoken language that images speak to themselves—first silently and then verbally through us—that compelling language moves us individually; it speaks to us in private ways according to our depth and our sagacity. But even when we lack the depth and sagacity to do with it what Scholes did, we respond nevertheless. We don't need Bob Scholes to tell us that Eugene Smith's photograph of Tomoko unsettles us, excites our love and concern; we don't need him to tell us that the sea stirs us, soothes and comforts and scares the bejesus out of us. We know intuitively of that compelling, collective power, that primordial power—the power that is itself a language.

ON SOME LEVEL, we respond to that unspoken language. We need neither education nor experience to be gripped. To understand is a more complicated matter. These days some may need

Scholes to link the sea's power to the Mother's, but back there in the sweep of time when less self-conscious folks *felt* more clearly than we do, one of them most assuredly felt the connection without anyone's help. One of them stood in awe of the sea and of the Mother and sensed a sameness; made a connection; began to make meaning, uttered words, drew a picture, perhaps. The sea took men away on adventures. I suspect it gave women insight. I imagine that a woman felt that connection first. Rhythms bound her and the sea together, told her of their sameness, led eventually to understanding. But the prelingual language behind the images—the binding power itself—was clear enough.

Now, in our time, all of us, men and women, have to draw pictures, talk, write . . . create the texts of our lives in whatever way we can. It takes a poet like e. e. cummings these days to remind us that "since feeling is first / who pays any attention / to the syntax of things / will never wholly kiss you." "Kisses," he tells us, "are a better fate than wisdom."

It is a fact, of course, that neither too much education nor too much conditioning can diminish the power of those primordial urges. And if we stop to think for even a moment, we know that when a poem or a novel or a movie manages to appropriate their power, when a text, any text, taps into it, we respond by saying "Yes!" We spend money for it, confirming it in our new, and often silent language of affirmation. We can't help ourselves; we are moved to do it. Eventually, the word gets around.

I don't have any idea when it was that I began actually to understand that prelingual language. Scholes reminded me of it that day in Seattle; the sea brought me back to it in the Caribbean, but I suspect I became aware of the language when I was in graduate school. I had grown weary of carrying around on my back the various professors who insisted that I see their way, that I write according to their formulas, that I confirm myself canonically. Sitting one day in my carrel in the university library, I read a sentence of E. M. Forster's that took hold of me. He described an aspect of the novel he calls prophecy, an aspect that has to do with reaching back in time, with a particular quality of voice, something akin to song. To illustrate his point, Forster chooses a scene from *Women in Love* "where one of the characters throws stones into the water at night to shatter the image of the moon." Forster tells us that Lawrence gets to the moon and the water by his own "special path which stamps them as more wonderful than any we can imagine. It is the prophet back where he started from, back where the rest of us are waiting by the edge of the pool, but with a power of re-creation and evocation we shall never possess." In other words, there really is a language besides the language I read; there is, as Forster says in an essay about Ibsen, something going on around the words themselves—something that may be more powerful than the words.

I left the mysterious matter of that other language in the back of my head for a few more years. But I relaxed, finally, confident, that I was not altogether out of my wits. And then, at thirty-eight, I wrote a sentence in an early chapter of my dissertation that stunned me. It was a sentence I had little to do with in any deliberate, conscious way. All of a sudden there it was before me, fully formed—a fairly long, complex sentence, lazy and graceful and full, a Newmanesque sentence, unlike anything I had ever written before, and it made perfectly good sense, something about a world intoxicated by growth and expansion, "the staggering of Empire" I called it, an English culture "gone berserk, drunk on the chilled white wine of rationality." I was placing a character's life against a cultural background, suggesting causal connections between psychic growth and cultural growth. It was a sentence whose meaning had little to do with its importance to me. That importance was embedded in the mysterious way in which the sentence formed itself and in David DeLaura's one-word comment in the margin. "Nice," he wrote.

No teacher in all my years of formal schooling had ever said that about one of my sentences. Suddenly at thirty-eight, fifteen or so years into an Army career, my life's priorities shifted. I began to think of myself as a writer.

Eight years earlier, I had been a teacher of writing, or so I thought. For three years, I had insisted that students at West Point write "five-paragraph essays," tightly organized, streamlined, somewhat insistent little pieces. That form of the essay calls for objectivity, a kind of scientific certitude. The essayist seems to stand aside from the controversy under consideration, examining it from just the right distance to have the final word. There is a certain predictability about this kind of essay. We may not know exactly what evidence writers will use to establish their case and how they will use that evidence, but we know from the promise in the beginning—from the thesis and the organizational suggestions—what general form the essay will take.

My mysteriously formed sentence and the work I was doing on my dissertation—the writing itself—suggested to me that I might have been doing myself and my students a disservice. I began to question the efficacy of emphasizing form—the five-paragraph form, the standard topic-sentence paragraph, any form—over exploration. I was, after all, completing a 600-page dissertation, working with only the most general sketch of how I would develop my piece. There were no notecards, no outlines for the construction of chapters, no preconceived conclusions; there was only a commitment to the task at hand, the inquiry itself. Somehow out of the chaos of all that generative activity, form took care of itself. That is not to say that my book-length manuscript fell into place as simply as the wonderful sentence did. It did not. But my imagination's logic served me well as I went along. By following what Sam Pickering would later call "the vagaries of my own willful curiosity," I discovered an order that made sense to me and to my readers.

When I went back into the composition classroom after graduate school, I was looking for a way to steer my students to a supple idea, something more akin to *notion* than to *thesis*. Not a simple declarative sentence promising proof but a more digressive invitation to the reader to participate in an excursion, an exploration, an inquiry. I wanted my students to discover that they can issue a different kind of invitation to their readers, an invitation to follow the twists and turns of an imagination discovering connections, making sense of life. I wanted them to know too that there's something about writing we can't account for altogether.

My own special sentence was there at the back of everything. Forster helped me understand how that sentence might have taken shape. In an essay called "Anonymity," he claims that "each human mind has two personalities, one on the surface, and one deep down." It's the lower one that really interests him. He claims that "unless a man dips a bucket down into it occasionally he cannot produce first-class work.... It has something in common with all other deeper personalities.... It is in any case the force that makes for anonymity.... The poet wrote the poem, no doubt, but he forgot himself while he wrote it, and we forget him while we read."

Jung sounds a bit like Forster when he insists that a true work of art is "supra-personal." He considers the creative process a "living thing planted in the human psyche," an *autonomous complex* that "leads a life of its own outside the hierarchy of consciousness." A writer can either submit to the process or struggle for conscious control; the one who lets go is likely to find the images and produce a true work of art. "Whoever speaks in primordial images," says Jung, "speaks with a thousand voices." The artist by giving the image shape "translates it into the language of the present, and so makes it possible for us to find our way back to the deepest springs of life."

When I went back into that composition classroom of my own, I had little more than a cherished conviction about autonomous complexes and a respect for the mystery. I knew there was something very important about writing that defied precise quantification. I knew about surrendering to the process. I had a sentence and a completed dissertation to prove it. The more I wrote, the more evidence I accumulated. Excited about letting go, it hadn't occurred to me in those days that the greater secret lay in the images.

The importance of images came to me first from other writers, from Joan Didion who theorizes about images that "shimmer"; from Loren Eiseley who insists that the writer does not have to impose a story on these pictures; the story is in the picture, waiting for the writer to discover it; from Toni Morrison who says that in her own writing she moves "from picture to meaning to text"; and from Virginia Woolf who believes that in the midst of life moments come to us that seem to be accompanied by a "sledge-hammer force." Those moments embed themselves in memory; they last.

Didion, Eiseley, Morrison, and Woolf point back to Jung and forward to James Hillman who reminds us that an image need not be perceived only "as a picture [that] can tend to become optical and intellectual and distanced." If we think of image as "context, mood, scene," we can enter it; we can be embraced by it. Hillman claims that "images hold us; we can be in the grip of an image. Indeed they can be gutsy." They have a life of their own. And now, I'm beginning to see, they also have a language of their own, a prelingual language that makes them speak to each other even before I can understand what they're saying in my imagination.

I BEGAN TO UNDERSTAND their language more clearly in my early 40s, after graduate school, when my father began to haunt me. I was driven by an insistent need to figure out how he had influenced my life even though he had never been around to influence me, and I got no relief until I listened to the incessant chattering of those images that bind the two of us together, even today.

When I sat down to write about my father, I had 5's on my mind, nothing else. At the beginning of my essay, I wanted to create a scene that would suggest what he might have given me through inheritance. I had discovered at seven that my father and I both made 5's starting from the bottom up. What interested me about the discovery was that my father didn't teach me how to make those 5's. That was the point I wanted to make. As I began creating the scene about the 5's, an image of separation came to mind, and I realized that I would have to use the two images together; they spoke to each other. One spoke of loss, telling how I shared, without understanding it, my mother's grief on the day she discovered that my father would leave her, and me. I was five when he left. The other scene would be about the 5's themselves, and it would suggest that my absent father continued to influence me long after he left home. As I wrote, those images of loss and gain led me to a scene in a honky-tonk in Fort Leonard Wood, Missouri, a place I visited only once in my life. When I walked in, sat there, and listened to the music, I became my father. The experience and the re-creation of that scene as I wrote, led me to yet another scene from my childhood, and before I knew it, I was following the vagaries of my own willful curiosity, creating an essay. I had begun with a single image about the 5's. I didn't know that I had any others at my disposal.

It was sometime later that I read Reynolds Price's *Kate Vaiden* and found the epigraph that I hoped would set my whole essay in motion for my readers: "(nobody under forty can believe how nearly *everything's* inherited)." But the essay actually outgrew that notion too; it became an inquiry into southern masculinity. It was male mythmaking I had on my mind when I started thinking about my father, and it was male mythmaking I had on my mind at the end, but I went a long way around to travel a short distance. Writing the essay, I had a feeling I was sailing on solar wind. I had chosen a general direction with a destination in mind, but I let the images lead me along; at the beginning, they seemed to know more about where I was going than I did. They had a life and a language of their own. They led me to my destination.

NOW THAT I KNOW MORE about the way images work and can be attentive to them, they tell me more than they used to. I guess you might say, I'm more open to them. I like their surprising intrusions. Last year, as I stood in my kitchen at Harvard making tea, my mother suddenly showed up. She had been dead four years, but she was there that morning as I poured the hot water over the tea bags. I could see her standing at her own stove, could see her pour the cream in her cup, see her eating her toast, preparing as she always was for work.

I liked the memory, was struck by it, and thought surely I'd use it in the mother essay I'd been trying to write since she died. But even though the memory and the experience of her that morning were packed with literary resonances—Proust, *la petite madeleine,* memory mingling with desire—I was not in its grip. The memory had little to do with my *idea* of her. I like to think too that my mom, working somewhere in my imagination, wouldn't allow me to use that image, literary as it was. Practically the last thing she told me, ever, was not to become too studious as I lived out my life. There's not much need for it out there, she said.

The essay I finally wrote was an essay about love, and it was a gesture of love that set it off, the mere touch of someone's hands on my face. As I began writing these sentences for "Goings and Comings," touch brought her back to me, took me first to her bedside in the nursing home and then back to my childhood: "I help her with her glasses, and as I push the frames back across her temples, she reaches up through the space between my arms and takes my face in her hands as she used to do when I was a little boy, holding me gently for a minute, then bringing her fingers down my cheeks, feeling as she does the shape of my face, confirming me by touch as her palms and then her fingers come together below my chin, the tips still touching the underside of my face, moving slightly from side to side, steadying both of us. Only her twitching lower lip betrays her steadfastness. Her eyes, she would say, are steady as the Rock of Gibraltar. But her voice won't work. I hear only deep, raspy guttural sounds."

In preparation for writing that essay, I collected books and scraps and articles—yessir, yessir three bags full—and not a single item found its way into the piece. I like to think she wouldn't tolerate them. After all, what does an essay about love have to do with scholarship? Not much I decided. Only an epigraph: "She is our history, and it is from her simple lap that we fell." The piece didn't seem to need any more decoration than that. What generated the essay was a reminder of her touch, her hands, their gentle power. That gesture, so representative of her, led me to others. Not long ago, as I sat in a theater watching *sex, lies, and videotape,* I thought of her again. Again an image did it. A man took a woman's hand, and the moviemakers gave us a long, leisurely look at the way those two pairs of hands spoke to one another, turning and touching, moving over the contours of faces desperate for love.

We know those gestures, all of us do; we know about those images; they move us; they grip us and speak to us in a language all their own. They speak to each other as well. But the images themselves do not tell the whole story. They move us, they link themselves, but they do not tell us straight out what they mean.

We have to translate the images, express them in language of our own. The images link themselves and move us to pay attention. When we do, we begin to understand our lives. We begin to have ideas that count.

AS I LAY THERE on the deck bench in the Caribbean, that flood of images had come to me—Conrad, the other books, the sea and sexuality, my dad and me on the fishing boat, William Carlos Williams and death. When I first recorded those images about a year after they rushed through my head, I was surprised by the way they clustered together, expressing much of what I had read and heard about the sea. But there in the middle of those recollections of secondary experience was one about me and my father, something primary, perhaps out of place in that cluster. That primary one intrigues me now as I look for ways to illustrate how these prelingual images bump up against one another and give us insight, how they speak through us.

The best I can figure, I was four years old when my family went on a trip to California with friends. I've heard others talk about the trip. No one else remembers my dad saying he would cut me up and use me as fish bait. My sister, who was eighteen years older than I, claims it didn't happen. But I recall being out on a fishing boat with lots of people. Perhaps it was a two-decker boat with a rail around it (that's how I see it in my mind's eye right now). People were fishing over the side, and I was too small to see much. My dad was standing there with four or five men, talking and laughing with them. He wasn't fishing. I must have been yanking on his pants leg, begging for something, because he picked me up, the way men toss children into the air, and he told me he would cut me up and use me for fish bait if I didn't settle down. I might have screamed and made a fuss, but I don't remember that. I remember only the way he laughed with the others about what he had said.

The image—the father threatening a young son in the company of other men, teasing and taunting him—reminds me of scores of stories I've read and heard, many of them from young writers trying to recreate learn-to-swim experiences, all of them about fear and recovery. But this memory of mine has stayed with me not as an image of fear and initiation, but as the only memory I have of me and my father together before he left home. I have thought of it only a few times in my life, but when I lay there on the deck bench in the Caribbean and was flooded with memories, that one came with the others. When I wrote those images down, my father came next in line after William Carlos Williams and death. I wrote that the experience with my dad scared me. But now, as I try to make sense of what happened, I doubt that I was so scared. I've never, as far as I know, had a dream about it. It didn't make me hate my father or resent him. It was the laughter and the teasing that I remember, and that laughter and teasing take me now to another memory, one that my sister gave me just a year or two ago.

I was trying to find out from her what I could about her own memories of our mom and my dad. I wanted to know what happened when Mom and Dad fell in love. Ellisene was about thirteen at the time, the middle child with two brothers. Mom still had the grocery store left her by Ellisene's father when he died. My dad worked in the store making deliveries. I had absolutely no clues about how the romance started between the widow woman who would become my mother and the much younger man, the marshal's son. Until Ellisene told her story I had been unwilling to imagine how such a relationship might have evolved. What she told me opened my mind to possibilities, giving me a new slant on him . . . and on myself.

The house that Mom and her children lived in—the one that would one day be my home too—had a spacious kitchen adjoining a bedroom across the back part of the house. Off that bedroom a sleeping porch extended out from the central structure of the house. The kitchen had an extension to its rear, a cozy breakfast nook with two benches off the walls on either side of a built-in table. The nook was a haven for children and adults to slide into, out of harm's way. The kitchen was modern before its time with cabinets all across one wall, floor to ceiling, lots of counters and a large porcelain sink with an extension for draining dishes, cleaning fish, making ice cream. On the other side of the kitchen, the side adjacent to the bedroom and a central bathroom, there was an arched, framed opening in the wall for the refrigerator; behind the refrigerator, additional storage space was accessible from a towel closet in the bathroom. Above the refrigerator a trapdoor provided access to an attic running across the whole house. Many years later, there would be pull-down stairs in the kitchen, but in those days entry to the attic was through the bathroom closet and up a ladder brought in for the occasion. I discovered that an agile boy might, with a little effort, shimmy up onto the refrigerator and then pull himself through the hole into the attic, leaving no trail behind of his whereabouts. It was a way to trunks and discarded treasures.

My dad, during the days of courtship, went up into the attic for a different reason. In the afternoons, when no one was home, he'd go to the house and cook. He liked to make big homemade cakes from scratch, liked to cook meals too. When mom was working and her children were away at school, he'd go into the house and prepare special treats for everyone. When he finished, near the time when the others would be coming home, he'd make his way up into the attic. Up there on the attic floor, above the kitchen, he'd make the most of an afternoon's work. Whatever he had done in the kitchen must have been very special because it stuck in the mind of a thirteen year old for a lifetime; more than fifty years later it was still Ellisene's primary memory of the wooing that took place there before her very eyes.

I like to imagine that young man in the kitchen, working by

himself, going through the cabinets, finding the right pots and pans, taking out the ingredients and mixing them, making himself at home. But I like best to imagine him hunkered in the attic, waiting for the laughter, waiting to hear the voices and the speculation, waiting for his own confirmation. I like to think about how long he stayed hidden, what made him decide to come down, what my mom said to him when he did. In my mind now, his joke, his gift, the laughter, remind me of the man who tossed me into the air and told me he'd cut me up and use me for fish bait. That's how I like to remember him.

But there on my back in the Caribbean, under the sea's influence, the image of me and my father presented itself in another context. He came to me in the context of death at a moment when I was exuberant over life. That flood of images spoke to me of the inextricable link between life and death . . . concluding with Williams's "Death is not the end of it." Only now am I beginning to understand the meaning. The images took me in tow, led me beyond the immediate experience of the sea. They spoke to me, as Scholes's images spoke to him, of life and death; they spoke to me, as they always do now, of the mystery of creation.

I know now that I can't always translate the images when they come to me; often I don't know enough or I haven't experienced enough in my own life to understand them. They tug on my spirit nevertheless, bidding me to pay attention.

IN MY CLASSROOM, I'm always interested in how images might play on my students' imaginations, how they might help those young, inexperienced writers make sense of experience. I have supplemented my notions about autonomous complexes with these notions about images, and I begin my writing courses by asking students to recover their own images of experience, to go back and find moments from their pasts that had some gripping power. Their discoveries always surprise me; rarely, if ever, am I disappointed with what they find. Always their image work has about it the scent of discovery; always, it seems to draw them to ideas they care about, ideas they want to express to their readers . . . and to themselves. They seem to enjoy listening to the prelingual language that binds those images together.

Sometime during the early part of all my classes, when I'm trying to get the students interested in the images, I turn to Annie Dillard's "Living Like Weasels." In that essay Dillard tells us about an encounter with a weasel that sent her writing. She looked into a weasel's eyes one day and was "stunned into stillness," she says. Her essay tells us why. At the outset, she gives us two glimpses of weasels; one socketed to the hand of a naturalist, the other fastened to the neck of an eagle. Dillard imagines the second having its "beautiful airborne bones" picked clean in flight. She is fascinated with the weasel's instinctive action and his tenacity even in the face of death, and her essay exhorts us to live like weasels, to hold on for a "dearer life," "yielding at every moment to the perfect freedom of single necessity."

I like that idea so much that I try often to help my students see where Dillard might have gotten it. I want them to see an image fit to die over, so I show them an actual weasel's skull, let them look at the fierce little head, cleaned and divested. I show it to them to shock them into awareness. I want them to be caught in the weasel's jaws, to see for themselves what it might be like to be seized by a single necessity, by an image so powerful they can't let go. I want them to imagine just for a moment what it might be like to be a weasel socketed and carried aloft, carried perhaps "as high as eagles."

I RARELY GO THAT HIGH, but often I get some sense of what it might be like—stretched out on the deck bench, behind the helm, looking up at the sails. I get some sense of what it might be like when suddenly I feel the tautness at the helm, the lift, the appreciable acceleration. It's the same feeling I had that afternoon in Seattle, lying on my back in bed, seized by the power of those images, thinking about them until I couldn't contain myself any longer. Images from Scholes's talk and other images from my life began to play against one another in my imagination, began to unsettle me, shake me up, rearrange my sense of life; they fastened onto me and wouldn't let go, and I had no other choice but to write. They took me back to the wellsprings of my life; they took me deep, close to the source itself.

Now . . . at long last, I'm beginning to understand the unspoken language of those images, and for a long, extended moment, they seem to be telling me all I need to know to get where I'm going.

The Spirit Was Willing and So Was the Flesh

In each of us the Spirit is manifested in one particular way, for some useful purpose.
CORINTHIANS 12

I HAVE A HERO'S TALE to tell and can't even begin to tell it straight. The ordinary facts of the tale have spun me round, turned my life back on itself time and time again so that now, I roll in a hoop of flame, spinning, looping, moving around and shooting forward, *dominus mobilis,* world without end. Amen.

Once in a very great while, when all movement stops, when my world quits spinning and I sit still inside it, suspended in my own imagination, quiet and submissive and alone, the ordinary facts of my life slide into place, images become patterns, and the tale begins.

THEY LIVED in an old farm house only a hundred yards off the paved highway in a little town called Snyder, Arkansas. I can't remember whether the boards of the house were bleached by the sun, or whether they were painted. But I do remember the porch across the front, a yard full of hound dogs, and the single picture I have of the five of them, posed together there on the steps in their Sunday best: my mom, her sister Kate, and their three brothers, Tom, Eb, and Simp. To the left of the house, way out to the left, beyond the hardpack of the yard and the fence itself, were the barn, the feeding troughs, the tractor shed, the hogs—and back behind it all, the fields of corn . . . and behind that even, the woods. To the right of the house, past the white oaks and the sweet gums, back through a rolling field, was the pond for the livestock and a place for Kate to fish. She went outside, to the porch or to the pond, for fun. Ernest, her husband, went deep in the woods, any woods, to the deer camp.

Out of the woods, in the fields and around the barns, out back in the smokehouse, Ernest worked, sunup till sundown, five and a half days a week, every week, except the two in the fall for deer camp. Even Kate would tell us near the end of his life, that he was staying alive for just one more hunting season. But there wasn't much else that meant more to him than Kate. Kate was enough, and for Kate, life with Ernest was enough.

Kate seemed to have her feet on the earth. She was a practical, hard-working, happy woman. When she and my mom were together, they laughed and laughed, loved each other so much I saw them crying tears of joy. I knew they were tears of joy, knew it as well as I knew the happiness on my mom's face in that picture of her and my dad on their wedding day. What Kate had for a lifetime with Ernest, and my mom had for most of the ten years my dad stuck around, was love so strong everything else made way for it, the kind of love you can't buy even if you move to town for it. It comes from inside, like God.

I saw a telling aspect of that love one night in that old farm house when I was a kid, saw it there in the bedroom in the dim glow of a coal oil lamp. That evening in the bedroom—Ernest in the rocking chair before the fire—Kate came in first with a washpan and then with two buckets, one just off the stove, both about half full of water. She had been at it all day. We had had a big breakfast—biscuits, eggs, grits, hot molasses, jellies, fresh bacon, milk, coffee for Ernest so strong I smelled it across the hallway in my room before I crawled out of the feather bed. Kate had made lunches for us to take to the field, had spent the rest of the day cleaning and canning, putting beans and peas and tomatoes up for the winter, and at the same time had made the pies and fixed our supper, had it piping hot when we came in from the fields.

So when she came into the bedroom and sat down on the hearth and began untying Ernest's boots, she was as tired as he was, plenty tired enough to sit in her own rocker and fall fast asleep, her socks down around her ankles, her hair frazzled, her body plumb wore out. Instead, she sat down on the floor beside Ernest and unlaced his boots, laughing and talking all the time. As he pulled his pants legs up over his shins out of the way, the cigarette he had rolled and licked shut was dangling from his lips as if it were a part of his face, curving limply, hooked and bent down like his nose. Kate had helped him out of his socks and poured water into the washpan, mixing the cold with the hot, careful to get it just right.

When Ernest put his feet in the pan, I could see the red-dirt stains dissolving, coloring the water as he swished around getting the warmth in between his toes. Kate poured more hot water and took the washcloth from her stack of linens. I remember watching her take it, placing it between her palms and making a ball of hands and cloth. In the pan, down under the water, she spread her hands apart, stretching the cloth between them, and then she raised and lowered the cloth into the water, up and down, up and down, taking it finally in a wad again and squeezing the warm water over first one leg and then the other as I watched the streaks running into the pan, watched her get the soap, watched her wash him clean. I don't know how long it lasted, that ritual, a long time it seemed, a long time of communion and laughter between a man and a woman in love.

Funny how I remember that house, that old man and woman, and I can't remember much about what happened in church before I went out there on Sundays for dinner and the family gathering. I never forgot the dinners and the washing, and neither did the others. I heard my mom say many times over the years, "She washed his feet every night of their lives." I don't know what else went on in that bedroom, don't know what Ernest did for Kate, but I do know they had a love that lasted, and their life was a sustaining ritual, sacred and earthy.

Almost thirty years after I saw Kate washing Ernest's feet, as I sat reading in my study about the Edwardians, I came across a line of Richard Ellmann's and understood immediately what he meant when he said the "transcendent is immanent in the earthy." Reading, I wondered again, as I had over the years, what had been going on with Christianity, why, as Forster might have said, there was no place in the Christian scheme of things for "decent carnality." It seemed to me, almost from the beginning of my time on earth, that the flesh and the spirit ought to be one. But someone, in another time, had decreed otherwise. Someone had seen fit to leave out a part of the mystery.

I think it was the church that confused me. It hadn't meant to put me in the back seat of that '53 Oldsmobile with the girl's mother in the front seat talking nonstop to another woman. But there I was anyway. I sat in the back seat with one of the daughters, and one of my friends was there too with the other daughter. It got dark on the way over to Parkdale, down those roads into the swamps and the bottomlands, and I began to notice how close her body was to mine. On the way back from the Methodist Youth Fellowship meeting, after the devotional and the folk dancing and the refreshments, we got into the Oldsmobile again, same places, and started home. It was there on the back seat of that car that I first became aware of a woman's body, what it felt like, what it could do to mine. I didn't have to do a thing. All I had to do was sit still, and it worked on me, stirred my spirit, set my imagination in motion. I believe that was the moment my soul woke up.

It would be a very long time, almost twenty years, before I got close to my soul, close to an understanding about her nature. At thirty-six, I read a book of Carl Jung's and began to see that there was indeed a woman in my head who had been there all along, from the very beginning, and that woman, my notion of her, has everything to do with my soul, my imagination, my life. She lives inside me, an image of my ideal woman, the one I'd most like to marry. Jung calls her *anima*. Once I knew of her existence, she told me things I needed to know to get on with my life.

Funny thing about that kind of knowledge too, what it does to you, how it helps you sort things out, no matter when it comes to you. Faced with the knowledge of anima, I began to tell myself stories I couldn't tell before. The first was a story about my wife, a story that suggests anima's power to lead men astray.

Ann, my wife, was crying out for "space." She was obsessed with images of flight, with travel, with going to Arkansas to care for her dad; she was anxious for old friends and for new, anxious for a way out of the cage I had been building around her for twelve years, subordinating her to the Army, to the organization that was claiming my life, subordinating her to the demands of my imagination, trying desperately to make her match the woman in my head, my idea of a woman who would love me the way I wanted to be loved. I began to see that I had been trying to remake Ann in the image of anima and as a result hadn't gotten to know either woman very well.

Meeting anima was a rude awakening. I had to face up to the fact that I had been under her influence without even knowing she had been moving me around. I found that I couldn't change my life until I learned more about that woman, her independence, and her life within mine.

I didn't have to wait long. Anima came right in. Nothing big. She showed up as an *idea* in a dream, something related to one of the stories in the book I was reading, *Man and His Symbols*.

Anima knocked on my door and said quite simply, I exist. Get to know me. Less than six months later, I wrote to the head of the English department at West Point and said, in essence, I have only one career in mind. I want to teach again. A week later, the dean called. Since then teaching and writing have occupied my life.

Anima doesn't appear very often in my dreams. She's only shown up four times, four times total in seventeen years, and yet ours has become a sacred relationship, something fit for the gods. Perhaps I exaggerate, but I don't think so. She is an archetype with ankles, as real to me as any woman I've ever known; she gives me insight into women I do know. In a strange way she invests those real women with spirit, transforming them before my very eyes into more than they seem. Sometimes she serves us well; sometimes not.

The second time anima showed up in one of my dreams, she appeared only from the waist up with the face of a woman who lived behind our house in Lee Area at West Point; the woman was a visiting professor in the psychology department. Managerial psychology was her business. She seemed driven the way a man might be driven by his profession. In my dream, her head was attached to a naked torso, whether hers or not I have no way of knowing. She appeared to me in profile, an icon, stylized, immobile, and nubile, her breasts small, erect, enticing, but they seemed too sexy on a woman I thought of as masculine.

When she came to me that night, I was still trying to understand my wife, and I assumed the dream was trying to tell me something about her. Ann and the neighbor seemed, on the surface of things, to share a strong, assertive personality. Both seemed to be in flight from someone else's notion of woman.

Now, I think the image had little to do with either woman. Anima came to tell me something about myself, not about my wife or my neighbor; anima came to me bearing news about the erotics of masculinity. She came to me at a time when I was suppressing my own sexuality, when I was trying to cope with life by living in a world of ideas, trying to draw spiritual sustenance out of a life of the mind. I had put my own body on hold, subordinating the flesh to an old masculine notion. I was in pursuit of spirit—a Pauline convert among the Corinthians. "I am absent in body, I am present in spirit," Paul had said. One or the other: body or spirit. According to Paul, the body could be nothing more than a "shrine of the indwelling spirit." And woman. Well, says Paul, "It is a good thing for a man to have nothing to do with women." But if he must, then he can marry as a concession. Better to sleep with one than with many. Better yet to be "as I am," Paul says.

I had not, of course, bought the whole epistle. The church, after all, had confused me when I was a kid. I had made that trip in the '53 Oldsmobile down those county roads to Parkdale, all under the auspices of the church. Perhaps I was forgetting the lessons of my youth. Whatever the case, that night at West Point down in Lee Area, anima came to remind me about the spirit, mine and hers. She came to resurrect my body. Like those biblical women, she seemed to be around at the right time. But I didn't know her well enough to understand her. Her image, as I've already said, can lead men astray. We can never be altogether sure about what she's telling us. That's why, I think, the patriarchs have for so long tried to keep her in her place—somewhere outside consciousness, in another room, perhaps, in a room not of her own choosing.

Once we let anima in, she moves us around, changes the way we see things. As fate would have it, she moves us around anyway. Yet once we recognize her, we too can begin to understand what's going on. That's the difference. We can begin to tell our stories.

To think of anima as only a dream woman is to limit her.

To make her a muse is to make her a fantasy. To see her only as a woman of the night is to place her in a compartment, in a room. She won't stand for it. Anima can save us or lead us to destruction. Ever present, tempting . . . our destroyer or our redeemer. We have to read her right to read ourselves. Tricky business. When she came to me the third time, I was still reading her wrong. I have a feeling, looking back, that she was getting impatient with me, so she sent me on a chase.

I had for a number of years been teaching a course called "Psychological Aspects of Modern British Literature," reading Conrad, Hardy, Forster, Lawrence, Woolf, and Lessing against a Jungian backdrop. Near the beginning of that course one year, the *New York Times* ran a feature article on Jim Hillman, who had for years been director of studies at the Jung Institute in Zurich. I decided to ask him if he would come to talk to my students. Eventually, he said yes. His wife, Pat Berry, head of training for the Inter-Regional Society of Jungian Analysts, urged him on. She wanted to see what was going on at the Military Academy.

They came and spent the night with us after his lecture. Over dinner, at some point, Jim told me about work he had done with the poet Robert Bly, trying to acquaint a group of men with anima. Jim used a tray of anima slides, everything from natural scenes that evoked pure mood to Playboy bunnies. As we talked I began to wonder what a tray of anima slides might contain if his wife Pat put them together.

That night at 2:15 A.M. I sat bolt upright in my bed having come face to face with anima for the first time. Two preeminent Jungians were down the hall, on the other side of the house. I wanted desperately to call out to them in the night.

Instead, I left them asleep and reentered my dream, following Pat out the back door of my house on the way to her car where she was going to get the anima slides. My dogs, a Welsh corgi

THE SPIRIT WAS WILLING

and a Great Pyrenees were with us, behind me slightly and to the right, between me and the house as we stepped off the porch onto the service road moving toward Pat's car. All of a sudden my dogs took off in hot pursuit of something around the corner of the house, barking as they headed down a slight incline in the direction of the Hudson River. I screamed for them to stop and ran to get them under control as Pat continued toward her car as if she had heard nothing. She left the dream. When I turned the corner, I saw anima, the dogs in pursuit. She was visible only from the waist up again, this time dressed in what seemed to be a deer skinjacket, soft, with fringe on the sleeves. Her back was to me as I rounded the corner; she was twenty yards ahead, and I saw only her jet black hair, shoulder length, hanging beautifully from her head. When I saw her, I left the ground, feet first, shooting toward her. When I got airborne, her head pivoted around as if she were an owl, and I found myself looking directly into the most beautiful black eyes I had ever seen. And there we were, in the air, face to face, she nothing but a head and a pair of eyes, eyes so powerful they had sat me straight up in bed at 2:15, jolted, my head awhirl, my body wet with sweat.

I wanted only to stay in the dream, wanted to keep reliving it, wanted to keep looking at her, trying to figure out what she was saying. At breakfast, Pat still upstairs somewhere, I told Jim the dream. He said, "The dogs are protecting your house, what's there and intact. She slammed you off your feet, and she's taking you across cultural boundaries, moving you across zones into something foreign, European, Indian, something like that, maybe." I walked into the kitchen and picked up an essay of Gretel Ehrlich's called "To Live in Two Worlds: Crow Fair and a Sun Dance." Ehrlich is a writer who lives on a 5,000-acre ranch in Wyoming.

There at the breakfast table, I showed Jim a couple of passages from "Two Worlds." Ehrlich claims that "we live in a culture that has lost its memory." Later in the essay, writing about a Kiowa sun dance, she gets to the bottom of our problem as she sees it: "Because Christians shaped our New World culture we've had to swallow an artificial division between what's sacred and what's profane." Even the Indians, she suggests, are culture straddlers, their feet in two camps, divided in their lives and divided in their consciousness, so divided they can no longer become "visionaries, diviners, or healers."

Jim made a note about the book, and said, "Yes, that's good. Something like that. You might be onto something." He left me with my dream.

The next day, I told my students what had happened. They laughed, pleased to see me stuck, and we went on with class, looking for vestiges of the spirit in modern British literature.

Conrad, in a funny way, was at the back of the course, the foundation for all that we were examining. I had, since my undergraduate days, been intrigued by Marlow's journey into the heart of darkness, baffled that he had to come back down the river to a more modern civilization only to tell a noble lie. He had to tell that lie about what he found in the darkness, he told himself, because Kurtz's "Intended" could not bear up under the truth of what had actually happened. Yet we know from his own story that he had gone on his journey under the influence of women, and having gone, he had found that at the very end of the river, in the heart of darkness itself, only the native woman with "helmeted head and tawny cheeks" stood silently in charge.

Despite his own evidence about woman's central place in the mystery of his journey, Marlow continues to think of himself as protector, continues to see all women as profoundly limited: "It's queer how out of touch with truth women are. They live in a world of their own, and there has never been anything like it, and never can be. It is too beautiful altogether, and if they were to set it up it would go to pieces before the first sunset." Caught up in his own storytelling, Marlow cannot see what Conrad saw. Only we, outside the frame of the story, can see, and even we are limited by our own patterns of perception.

Marlow's problem is our own. How to read our lives in the clearest light—a light that may very well shine out of our own dark interior. Pat Berry, whom I should have asked about my dream that night in New York, suggests that we usually tell our stories too straight because our "ego is [always] close at hand." Telling dreams is like telling stories. The hero finds himself in the middle of his own dream, and imposes a false order on the tale, severing just those aspects of the "dream image" that he is trying to bring together. There is another way to meaning, Pat reminds us. We can "view the tale as archetypal"; when we do, we and our characters represent far more than our own narrow viewpoints. If we turn ourselves over to the images, they might very well shape us and change the shape of our stories—those stories we tell ourselves in order to live.

My third woman, that woman with the severed head and the black eyes, led me finally to Colorado. When I set out to help a friend die, I had forgotten about the woman in my dream. But on that trip, anima turned the ordinary facts of my life back on themselves. She set me up and sent me deep within myself.

Bobbie and I had met fourteen years earlier in Oklahoma, and we had let our imaginations take fire from one another's. Her imagination was reckless and deadly serious in its carefree search for spirit, for any morsel of life she could take from me, from books, from her art, or from her other friends. She was an artist, not yet accomplished. I was a career Army officer. We were never lovers, but we loved each other dearly.

Over time, following those years in Oklahoma when she, Roger, Ann, and I were all together at Fort Sill, Bobbie would call, usually at two in the morning. When we talked, everything seemed possible. We transformed ourselves in the darkness of the night when no one else seemed to care. She called always out of some restless need. The restlessness, I always suspected, came from wanting life whole—wanting it desperately. She knew about human limitations but couldn't bear to be shackled by them. She thought and talked about spirit—read, meditated, prayed, painted, yearned, yearned always for something in this life that would give her insight into the other.

When she painted the Indian chiefs in Oklahoma, she painted to close in on them and their life. But what she painted fell short of what she felt. No one knew that better than Bobbie. What she wanted to paint in those days but couldn't was the Indian's masculine, spiritual power. That's what she wanted to get hold of. She was a Catholic through and through. Men held the keys to the kingdom. Mad as Bobbie was for spirituality, she could never quite see herself as source, could never see that she, a woman, had been invested with the power. She called at two in the morning because she thought I might have it; she called to talk about the women I had been reading and to tell me about other women—her friends, her fellow artists. What she needed and wanted was masculine consecration. So we exchanged energy, diminished the distance between New York and Colorado, suspended willingly our disbelief in this life.

When Bobbie called one Saturday afternoon, fourteen years into a friendship, I was troubled as I stood in our kitchen waiting for Ann to finish talking. Bobbie had never called in the afternoon.

At first, her voice sounded fine, same as always—husky, full of life, untamed. She had just come back from Hawaii, celebrating her fortieth birthday with Peggy, her twin sister. It had been glorious; it had been wonderful . . . but as she got past the surface details, past the trip itself, her voice lost its luster.

"I don't want y'all to worry, but my arms are tired, and I can't work very long." And then the optimism. "Everything's going to be all right. Roger's helping me."

"Bobbie?"

"Everything's fine."

A week later, she gave us the news. Amyotrophic lateral sclerosis (ALS), Lou Gehrig's disease.

A month later, she was in a coma, the result of neglect during a CAT scan. Two months later, she opened her eyes but had no voice.

ALS destroys the motor neurons in the brain that control the muscles, robbing the body of strength, control, and oxygen. The lungs shut down. But the brain remains intact, unimpaired. Bobbie's muscles deteriorated rapidly beyond recovery, but she was being kept alive by a respirator—by the wonders of modern technology and a legal system unable to deliver the death she craved.

Bobbie knew that she had won the prestigious "Purchase Award" from the Pastel Society of America, knew that Damon would graduate in a few weeks, knew that smiling Jason lived in pain, that Roger struggled to hold the pieces together. She knew her life's work was finished. But she couldn't talk about it. She had no voice. For all intents and purposes, she was a pair of blinking eyes. After a while she couldn't blink; only changes of expression around her eyes relayed her feelings. For eight months, at home, bedridden with round-the-clock nurses, virtually disembodied, she waited for the courts.

A letter from Roger finally robbed me of my optimism. I saw clearly that there would be no recovery, that even Bobbie couldn't beat the odds. Fearing I might upset the family routine by going at an inappropriate time, I called Bobbie's friend Ala before I called Roger. He would insist on my coming even if he knew I shouldn't. Ala had dialed the phone for Bobbie the last time she called me, before the coma. They were sisters of imagination, and I knew Ala would know Bobbie's state of mind. I trusted her.

"Pat," Ala said, "you have to decide. It'll be alright if you come. Don't worry."

A week later on the plane, I began to review my plans. I had a satchel full of books and papers, pieces I imagined Bobbie would like to hear. I wanted to face death with her. I even let myself think that I might be able to overrule the courts and let her die peacefully. I would be the agent of death because she would want me to be. Inflated, in the air over Kansas, I changed from brooding procrastinator to swaggering hero. I had duties to perform.

As I waited out my time on the plane, my mind wandered. Searching the past, I listened to Bobbie's voice justifying the time she spent painting. The bickering between her and Roger over art and familial responsibilities seemed trivial. I remembered those early paintings from Oklahoma, sketches of the Meers Store and the oils of the Indian chiefs. As I did, I paused a second over my earlier dream but moved quickly past what seemed a tenuous connection.

Back on the ground, I felt relieved for some reason, anxious to get on with my journey, anxious to see what I could do for Bobbie. My agenda set, all I had to do was find Ala.

Driving down the rain-soaked highway, I had the feeling I was sitting on top of the world, in charge. I had a plan and knew where I was headed. But when I came to the turnoff to Elizabeth, the little town where Bobbie and Roger lived, I got the shock of my life. The sign pointing me left, said "Kiowa 13." The hair on my head shot straight up.

I had to go through Kiowa to get to Bobbie. I had to deal with the Indians.

After turning onto the main street in Elizabeth, I pulled the car into the dark between the two trees and walked up to the front door of what had been the old bank building. I saw their sign: *The Steppe Sisters*. On the door, Ala had left a note, a patch of brushstrokes, a rainbow, under which she had written, "Pat, I'm next door at Halls—Come & get me—Ala. P.S. Sorry it's raining, I didn't mean it."

At Halls, the five women were waiting for me at a table of their own. When I walked in, they rose to greet me, hugged me each in turn, and motioned me to join them. They checked me out as if they'd been looking for me all my life.

"Can I get you a drink?" Ala asked.

"I'll get it," I said as I tried to stand.

"Scotch?" she asked.

"Yes, please."

My head was buzzing. I was being taken in. I felt it, felt their imaginations playing over me, knew that I had to say something to get relief when Ala walked back to the table with my drink.

"I'm in a strange frame of mind," I offered.

"Tell us about it," they said.

"I've got things Indian on my mind. It's weird. Coming here, turning off toward Kiowa, I was stunned."

"Do you know about the ceremony?" one of them asked.

"What ceremony?"

"The one the Kiowa's performed for Bobbie. They came all the way from Oklahoma, the ones she used to paint, her friends. They came and held a service for her."

"You're kidding," I said.

"All during the service, an eagle flew over, hovering," one of the sisters said.

Ala said, "I looked at Bobbie during the ceremony, in her chair out in the sunshine and the fresh air and asked if she were the eagle. She blinked yes."

I looked around the table, watched them looking at each

other, waiting for me to say something. I told them my dream about the dark-haired woman with the black eyes. The Indian woman who was only a severed head. They smiled.

"Did you know that Bobbie's Indian sign is the deer?" a friend named Barbara asked.

I told them my student's story about his mother's death, the story I'd brought to read to Bobbie. It was about his mother's spirit inhabiting a deer.

"It's time to go," Ala said when I finished the story.

Roger greeted us, smiling but fidgety. I was still reeling from the women's mysteries and had lost my swagger, lost my sense of direction, knew only that the time had come to face Bobbie.

We were led down the stairs by the sound of the respirator into a big room that had been partitioned to create privacy. Bobbie lay in her room on the bed amidst the tubes; the machine pulled and pushed on her, giving her life she had not chosen. As we stood there by her bed, Ala on one side, me on the other, Bobbie opened her eyes and looked first to Ala.

"Pat's here," Ala said.

Very slowly, as if it took centuries, Bobbie moved her eyes over to greet me, and I could see movement under her brows. I bent down to kiss her and did my best to hug the inert body. I told her I loved her. I knew she was struggling, just as I was, so I told her I would be back in the morning to read to her. She closed her eyes and left us alone.

The next morning, Sunday, upstairs over her room, I woke early, hoping to be alone again. I wanted to look out in the backyard on the only view she could see from her basement window. On pretty days, they rolled her outside. That morning was cold and damp and gray. A couple of birds flitted about and the wind played over the grass. I turned back to my bag and to the papers and books I had brought to read.

After breakfast I went downstairs. Roger had cleared the way and left us by ourselves. Bobbie was wide-eyed and alert. I told her what I wanted to do but didn't tell her why. I began with D. H. Lawrence's "Song of Death":

> Sing the song of death, oh sing it!
> For without the song of death, the song of life
> becomes pointless and silly.
>
> Sing then the song of death, and the longest journey
> and what the soul carries with him, and what he leaves behind
> and how he finds the darkness that enfolds him into utter peace
> at last, at last, beyond innumerable seas.

Her eyes were still open, wider perhaps, smooth under her brows, saying read me more . . . or so I thought. I turned to the piece about the deer and read the whole thing. Her eyes said continue, so I tried to lighten the mood with a short piece about my family. As I began reading, I looked over at her, and her eyes were closed. I stopped reading. She opened her eyes. She didn't want to hear about *this* life.

I turned then to Annie Dillard's "Living Like Weasels." I knew the piece almost by heart, so I could watch her reaction. As I read, Bobbie's eyes grew intense, and I could see movement under her brows as her eyes danced. When I came to the ending, she was more alert than I had seen her since my arrival:

> I think it would be well, and proper, and obedient, and pure to grasp your one necessity and not let it go, to dangle from it limp wherever it takes you. Then even death, where you're going no matter how you live, cannot you part. Seize it and let it seize you up aloft even, till your eyes burn out and drop; let your murky flesh fall off in shreds, and let your very bones unhinge and scatter, loosened over fields, over fields and woods, lightly, thoughtless, from any height at all, from as high as eagles.

From as high as eagles, I thought as I looked over at her face and saw a single tear roll from the corner of her eye and follow her nose, slowly, all the way down to her lips. I bent over, kissed her saltiness, and said goodbye.

Back at the bank building, Ala was waiting for me. When I walked in, she welcomed me and gave me free rein to see the work she had been doing under the influence of Bobbie's spirit. There were two huge paintings on opposite walls, two from a series of four. The one that arrested me was called "Guardian of the Door: Force."

A woman stands in the center of the framed space, winged with a canopy that rises up from her back and extends across the space from border to border. She is naked but draped, a flowing shoulder scarf covers her left breast and crosses the thigh of one leg, covering the other. The exposed leg, bent and pointing to her left seems to rest easily on a ferocious beast who stares straight out of the painting. The woman's sacred space, covered by the scarf, is at the very center of the picture. We must imagine what is behind the scarf. Her right breast and arm are exposed, and a thin striation, a trace of blood perhaps, arcs up from the naked breast, joining the arc of the winged canopy. Guardian's eyes look off to her right, out of the painting. Commandingly beautiful, she brings us round behind, beckons us to enter the kingdom she guards. Even the fierce beast at her feet, her foundation, her pedestal of power . . . even he submits. Not he but she, that is the point. *She* is the guardian.

I turned to Ala and smiled. She drew the shade, took a small bowl of shavings and incense, and brought a flame into being, fanned smoke into my hair, blessed my travels, hugged me, and sent me reluctantly on my way back to New York, back to West Point to initiate young men and women into life, to teach them to be heroic.

In my office the next morning, sitting alone with my thoughts, I listened again to what Ala had told me. They had welcomed me as Bobbie's guest; they had known, all of the women had known, about our souls. Before Bobbie's sickness, they had planned for me to come, had planned to take me into the mountains to their favorite spot, to feed me strawberries and drink champagne with me. And then they planned to leave me in that sacred space, alone, planned to leave me there in the plenitude of the earth so that I could experience what they experience, time and again. That is what they had planned and laughed about together. My coming to Colorado was not to be for death; it was to be for life.

Sitting there in my office at West Point, thinking about the women, I joined them, lost myself, became them for a while, for a long, long time it seemed, longer than I had ever been anywhere before. I sat there, down in my own space, out of mind into regions so deep I knew not where I was, into a quietness, into a lacuna in my soul.

The rapping on my door seemed faint and remote at first, an intrusion from another world I did not know anymore. It was an insistent rapping that finally became a pounding, and my friend from that other world opened the door and told me news so bad about one of my students that I rose to the words, to the challenge, traveled up a spiral out of my depths and stood erect, ready to strike out at the man who had said of my student's paper, "We can't consider it for this contest. It's brilliant, but the subject isn't appropriate. It wouldn't do for the department to select it as a winner." I had been called back to the other world, ready to fight, like a man.

It had been a long journey from that dream about the Indian woman—the first time anima had jerked me around and sent me into the future. She had led me to Colorado, set me up for the trip, and although I went I was reluctant to see that her powers extend to the future. I didn't want to believe that she could be outside my head, that I could find her in a bed, a severed head, that I could find her in a painting that had already been painted before I saw her, that she could lead me into the depth of my soul, taking me altogether away from my self-proclaimed, swaggering grandeur. I just didn't want to know that she could indeed slam me off my feet as Jim Hillman had suggested. In a dream, perhaps. In life . . . well, I had to sit there deep inside myself in that office that day, to find her out, to find myself.

AS I BEGAN TO FIND anima outside myself, she showed up that night in the honky-tonk near Fort Leonard Wood. Whirling around a dance floor, she captured my attention. I wanted to dance with her. Standing there watching her, I knew for the first time in my life what it might have been like to be my father— a man who died far too young from chasing images he didn't understand. When anima led me to my father that night, I had to tell the story of our lives, mine and his and hers. It was the first real essay I ever wrote. It signaled a marriage of sorts, a marriage between anima and animus: the masculine part of my psyche—the part that gives me distance from mood—marrying the woman in me. Animus had been on a long rest, watching anima have her say, I suppose. He came out to join her.

The surest sign those two had married up in my psyche came when I saw *Phantom of the Opera,* a musical about a sacred union—animus and anima in *coniunctio,* the divine syzygy—a musical about how the male spirit can invade the female, how Phantom can love a woman into helping him make music. It is yet another version of the old story about the muses. But with a twist. The woman doesn't serve Phantom subserviently; he too muses, sings his yearning, utters his plea for help, knows that he can't make music without her, yet knows as well that he has the power to woo her. Helping him, she *and* he will gain a new musical life. That's the alluring promise, his need and hers. Enter into a partnership, surrender, he urges her.

> Open up your mind
> Let your fantasies unwind. . . .

> Touch me, trust me, savor each sensation
> Let the dream begin, let your darker side give in
> You alone can make my song take flight
> Help me make the Music of the Night.

I wanted to be Phantom. Behind his mask, I saw myself. I too could sing my song. I bought the button, bought the T-shirt, bought the music, and for a year dressed myself in black against the coldness of the night.

Phantom eventually brought me a dream. In that dream, I, Phantom, embraced Anima, took her for my wedded wife, held her to my heart, faced her, and bounced with her down the stairs to the bass rhythms of my song. Dum, dum, dum, dum... down into the darkness of the night.

But there is more. To recognize myself behind the mask and in my dream is not to be Phantom. Recognition is but an inclination in the right direction; seeing is not believing. Anima has moved my spirit, slammed me off my feet, stirred my life. Because of her I am freer, less guarded, closer to life's mysteries. She comes bearing gifts even when I do not bid her. But accepting her gifts, understanding them, letting them shape the life that I live—that is another matter.

Not to sleep the dream, not to make waste of the spirit, not to seek the spiritual outside and apart from the life that I live, that, I think, is my sacred task. That is what Ellmann, Kate and Ernest, Bobbie, Ala, and anima have been trying to tell me. Were Jim Hillman here at this moment, I suspect he would remind me that I am fortunate to be "metaphorical man... always at sea, always en route between, always in two places at once." That's where I want to be, in two places at once—not suspended, but moving back and forth, at ease, open always to this life and its immanent mysteries.

I look back to Kate, back to Ernest, and I wonder. I wonder what else they could tell me about love that I haven't learned.

Phantom and Anima would puzzle them for sure if I tried to explain the sacred pair, but I'll just bet if they heard the music, they'd know; they'd know too just how much more there is left to tell in this hero's tale.

AS I SIT HERE THINKING of anima, I no longer see myself confined within the world—spinning, whirling, and looping around, searching restlessly for deeds to perform. She has calmed me, given me promise, taken me outside that lordly self, given me another view, taken me onto the top of the world itself where we lie down together.

As we move, the world spins still beneath us. We too are still in the earth's rotation, creating our own motion. We are the music; we are the thing itself. As I enter her sacred space, our bodies move in and against one another. On top of her and in her, beneath her, her on top in me, atop the *axis mundi*, we make angels together in the snow, here on the polar ice cap. She, next to the very earth, moves her arms in arcs, spreading her legs and closing them around me or under me as she wills, and then we turn, roll over, she on top, me on bottom again, moving from angel-making to angel-making in our field of snow, forming them, linking them, aglow from our own heat, loving and holding and rolling, we know the peace that passeth understanding.

World without end. Amen.

Mortality

And think of me until I too can go
Into the only world the heart would ever know.
DAVID MIDDLETON

THE SCENT OF DEATH drew me to the keyboard this morning. Today is Saturday, November 10, 1990, the day after my younger son's twenty-fourth birthday, the day Ellisene called. Before Mom died, Ellisene waited for my calls. On her birthday we'd laugh about getting old. As we did, I'd think to myself that only she, my older sister, was aging—and not much at that. Now, at fifty-one, I have a different perspective. We aren't exactly spring chickens. Neither of us. These days, her eighteen-year edge seems inconsequential as I ponder my own mortality. Life is upon us. And death.

I TRIED TO EXPLAIN something of the joys of growing old to a young Harvard student the other day. He had stopped by my open door to chat. I had aging on my mind and told him. He laughed and said his dad is a little touchy about the subject. I'm not. I like waking up every day to a routine that sprinkles hairs all over my sink. I stand there brushing and then shaving, performing my ablutions, and find hope in the whiskers; they keep growing and I keep cutting. But the hair on my head falls out of its own accord, checking me, reminding me of my years. In the mirror I see a shifting mass. I'm veering in the direction of portly, but my life of moderation has kept me trim, and I expect a lifetime's habits will hold me steady. I'm banking on it.

That's what Charles has been doing too. Banking on steady.

He and Ellisene married some forty years ago. I must have been eight or so and had been spoiled by an older, adoring sister. Charles has never been one to let me forget that fact, or the fact that I went to visit them the week after they came back from their wedding trip, and every summer thereafter until they moved in with Mom and me for a few years. Eventually they built a house next door, and now that Mom has died their house is the only one left. Mom's was sold and moved across town. Now, Ellisene's house sits at the center of three lots. The land and their house—and Ellisene and Charles themselves—span my waking life; they remind me each time I go back to Arkansas just exactly where I've come from. I take my bearing from them, try to figure out where I'm headed. My values were formed in Hamburg, and they continue to shape me and hold me fast.

I recall the years before Charles, the war years, when Ellisene and her friends had their parties up in the living room of our house. I don't actually know whether she knew Charles then. He was from Monticello, another small town thirty miles up the road. I had been born there because that's where the doctor was. All her life, Mom would tell me about Johnny Price's hands, hands that had taken me at knifepoint from her forty-three-year-old womb, delivered me to her. As far as she was concerned, J.P. was the finest surgeon in seven states. He performed miracles, brought life into the world and sustained it all over south Arkansas.

During the war years, all the men in my family gone and many of the men in our community away in the service, I could walk from my sister's bedroom directly into one of her parties in the living room. No one seemed to mind me. When I'd wander in, Ellisene would sit down, hold me in her lap, and let me watch the others dance—her friends and the soldier boys who had driven up from Selman Field down in Louisiana, some sixty miles away. I suppose some of the local boys had been lucky enough to get

Selman Field as their place of duty and brought the others home. The buses, as many as fifteen a day, kept Mom busy at the bus station. She met them all and looked upon each of the soldiers as her own. Some of them made their way to our house over those years. Only forty or so miles away, near McGhee, there was a Japanese internment camp. The war was everywhere, right on our own doorstep, disrupting lives and changing circumstance.

One time, in the afternoon when I should have been napping, Ellisene and Doris Morgan and Ann Etheridge and maybe Dot Holman were in the living room with two black women listening to the Andrew Sisters and boogie-woogie music. The black women were teaching the others to do the Camel Walk, a dance that had all of them in stitches as first one and then the other of my sister's friends took her turn on the floor trying to imitate the moves: shuffling forward, walking funny while moving first one shoulder down—finger pointing to the floor—and then the other, all the time swinging their hips from side-to-side, as natural as breathing, in time with the music. The white women were trying to learn what the black women knew. I was peeping from behind a chair pushed aside for the lesson. No one noticed.

Back then, I didn't know much about what was going on. I see now that they were coping, their lives disrupted by war. Our two brothers—like Charles—were gone, Willard headed for Cairo, Dub for England and death in a flak-filled sky over Germany, yanked from a gunner's turret where he had been sitting, waiting, uncertain about whether he'd be blown to bits or plummet to the earth. Hovering in the turret against the cold of those missions, he must have been thinking about that living room on Parker Avenue in Hamburg, Arkansas, thinking about whether he'd ever come back and join the rest of us for life. The odds beat him. In the meantime, the rest found a way to survive. The women and the stateside soldiers danced the hours away, laughing when they could, waiting. At night, I watched their fun. During most of the days, Ellisene worked for the rationing board.

Charles came back. So did Willard. Dub did not, and Dot Holman had to make a fresh start. Ann Etheridge found Billy Veazey. Ellisene found Charles. The two Hamburg women found the two men who had grown up in Monticello, walking the dirt paths together until the war had jerked them apart. To this day all of the living remain best of friends; they share weekly, sometimes daily, rituals: swapping yarns, playing bridge (still), riding to Monroe, Lake Village, Little Rock . . . just to eat. Nothing, it seems, but time and circumstance can rip them apart.

When Ellisene called this morning, I wasn't surprised. It was Saturday, and she was steady as the clock. Not much different from Charles, who as far as I could tell, hadn't missed a beat in their forty-odd years together. He was seventy on his last birthday. Cancer had paid him a visit a little over a year before, but even then, he was up and at it in a short time, walking his three miles around town every morning and spending much of his day in the workshop out behind their house where he makes furniture, mostly on order from people around town. His dad had owned a sawmill, and Charles had once worked for him, scaling logs, working deep in rattlesnake-infested woods. Later in life Charles turned rough logs into lumber and then turned scraps into pallets; he was the foreman of another man's mill. The life Charles loves and lives is close to the earth. He never left those woods altogether, and yet he is a gentleman, almost urbane at times. Dressed and ready for church, he might tell a story in a voice so mellifluous you'd think you were listening to J. William Fulbright working a deal on a smart but outclassed Patrick Moynihan. Charles is no politician, but he is shrewd, keeping his own counsel except behind closed doors, never raising his voice even there. When he retired a few years ago, the workshop steadied his life. He loves possessing the wood, savors the drying stacks of rough lumber out under the eaves of his shop, enjoys dressing and then shaping those boards, creating from them something lasting. In the shop he gets his hands on the wood, and I imagine the feel of it takes him about as close to his father as he can stand to get.

There's only one other thing that takes up as much of Charles's energy as the shop. He and Ellisene mow the yard together, once a week, always on the same day, always the same way. Over the years, they've developed a routine that involves teamwork and cooperation, sweat and patience. They used to work with push mowers, but the job got too big when they took on Mom's lot and then the adjacent lot that was vacated when the town finally dismantled the Legion Hut. All the land belongs to Ellisene and Charles now, and they take pride in the clearing they've done, the trees they've planted, even the transplanting they did to save Mom's spirea bushes when the movers came for the house. Everyone in town knows about their passion for the yard, and when Charles was sick last year, neighbors and friends came to control the growth until he and Ellisene could get back home. Just a month ago, the old post oak tree on the Legion Hut lot died, and the two of them did most of the cutting and hauling to restore the lot to its sculpted beauty. Their investment in the work sustains them from week to week, marks their steady progress against the vicissitudes of nature. They groom the yard, raking and cutting, noting the changes but holding their own. Steady.

When Ellisene called this morning, I was in the laundry room doing wash. I had just pulled the switch to start the motor when the phone rang.

"Did I get you up?"

"No, hardly. I've been up a while, but haven't been talking."

"I'm sorry to tell you, I've got bad news," she said, her voice cracking.

"Is it Charles?"

"Yes," she said fighting back the tears, "it's in his lungs and liver and lymph glands, and they've started the chemo."

"Oh, God," I muttered. I still couldn't talk. My voice wouldn't work. But there was a rush of feeling, a deep-seated welling up of memory, even as I sat on the edge of the old chair in the basement, listening to her trying to tell me what was on their minds.

"He has so much to teach me," she said. "I worry already about the simplest things. How to sharpen the blades on the lawn mower, things like that. . . . He's doing pretty well, still goes to the shop every morning. Say a prayer for us, hear?"

After I hung up, I went back into the laundry room and poured detergent down into the swirling water. Ellisene's call had interrupted my morning activities. I was doing a few chores before going to my office to write. It's a new routine in a middle-aged life—one I love and depend on for my own survival.

As I walked away from the washing machine, I had a compelling need to talk to Mom who's been dead going on five years. The need comes on me strong, involuntarily. The last time it happened I wanted understanding. I knew for certain that no one else in the world could follow the twists and turns of my mind except her. And so I needed to talk with her . . . and did. She was there on the other end of the conversation, reminding me that everything would be fine. That's what she always said, "Everything will be fine, don't worry." I suspect she had told herself the same thing so many times and found it true that she could say it with a lifetime of conviction. Anyone listening to her would be compelled to agree, not by her efforts, but by her voice, the way she said it. I wanted to hear her say it about Charles, and about Ellisene who would eventually be alone for the first time in more than forty years. I wanted to know that I would be fine too.

I walked back up to the living room with a basket of clean

clothes and began instinctively to fold them. I always fold them the same way, fold the towels in half and then in half again and then again. But I fold the face towels and the washcloths in thirds, the way they hang in the bathroom. As I worked, I stacked towels and cloths together and set them beside my underwear, folded the way I'd had to fold it at West Point, except there we had to wrap it around paper inserts so that the folds would be neat and the lines of the stacks clean and orderly, sitting on the locker shelves, assuring anyone who cared to look that our soldiers' world was in apple-pie order. If we could line up underwear, we could line up the troops. We could perform necessary tasks with exacting precision. Doing so, we could make things last. The lining up I learned from someone else a long time ago, but the instinctive folding came upon me involuntarily this morning.

As I folded and stacked, I was struggling to hold on, and for a while, the work helped. Sitting on the sofa, my mind drifted to the corners on the bedsheets. I like making the complicated tucks at the foot of the bed. The angle of the fold is there, the tautness, the complication, the perfection. I make a tuck in about three seconds.

Ann, my wife, talks a lot about the little things in life, how much they count. Part of her running commentary is designed to raise my awareness, but as I moved around this morning, doing the washing and straightening and folding, I began to see how much the doer gains from those daily chores. For an hour or two I turned myself and my suffering over to the ritual, and it sustained me. But the work itself, or the quietness in the house, or some deep-seated mechanism in my psyche also seemed to be helping me along, generating images, all of those images that I've already written down in this essay. They came unbidden and spoke to me of survival. They spoke of loss and gain, steadiness and ritual. They spoke too of life and death.

A couple of years ago on that pack trip in Wyoming, I had a

chance to ride directly behind the nine packhorses that were tied together and strung out behind the wrangler at the head of the column. There behind the trailing sorrel in the pack train, I could watch her take up and preserve the other horses' rhythm. After a watering break in a fairly deep creekbed, the wrangler had to take the lead horse straight up the steep bank and onto the trail. Each horse had to jump up from creek to land. By the time the first two or three horses had their footing and had begun to settle into the climb, the others were being yanked around a bit; they were growing tense, snorting, becoming skittish. As each found its way, in turn, up onto the path, only the sorrel remained in the creekbed at the end of the rope. She wasn't there alone more than five seconds, but it seemed an eternity as I watched her body and her movements adjusting to the thrill and excitement of the pull. Sliding on the shale of the creekbed, clomping about, she lept, at last, at just the right moment to release the others, giving them the slack they needed to climb on up the steep trail leading to Wall Mountain. My horse followed the sorrel's lead. All the rest of us seemed tied to them.

When I sit at the keyboard writing, I too seem to be following a lead to higher ground. The unbidden images pull me roundabout, stir my spirit, lead me along a trail of discovery. Turning those images into words, I am transformed, shored up against the flux of daily life that swirls around me. In the grip of the images, I sit still and write, and on occasion they give me reassuring glimpses into faraway places where I've never been.

A year ago on our sailing trip in the British Virgin Islands, I awoke very early in the morning from a dream. In the dream, I was in a New York apartment building, high up, as the building began to disintegrate. Here is what I wrote in my journal: "the building seems to fracture, breaks into cubes that seem to be losing their relationship one to another. I am somehow responsible for bringing things back together. I am not outside this experience watching it. I *am* the experience. When the building breaks up, I am on one of the blocks (that seems to be left in place pivoting about a rod as our stove pivots in the ship even as we rock). The block swings, and as it does I experience the swinging and the sensation of height. My job seems to be to re-pin the blocks together, to make the structure whole again." My first thought on waking from this dream in the forecabin was to see the movement of the building blocks as part and parcel of the sea's movement: a part of the natural rhythm of life. I was exhausted but pleased by what the dream seemed to be telling me about my role as preserver. In the midst of chaos, I have a natural instinct for reestablishing order, for finding a way. Even my dream images orient me, hold me steady.

Virginia Woolf, who sits close to my mind as I write, believed that the "whole world is a work of art." Occasionally, after moments of emotional intensity, Woolf glimpsed a "pattern" behind the "cotton-wool of daily life." She had a sense of how we fit into that pattern. During those moments of insight she depended on her "intuition." What she saw, she said, seemed to be "given to me, not made by me." This morning after Ellisene called, I saw what Woolf meant. The images seemed given to me, and I couldn't help wondering where they came from. Trailing one another, they seemed to be pulled from my psyche by some unknown force, linked by an invisible thread holding them in tow.

Often an image will come to mind when I'm writing a particular essay, and I won't know what to do with it. That image of the horses came as I was writing an essay called "Soldiering." Trying to find a way to move the essay's story from the flatland of Cub Creek up to the Continental Divide, I stumbled across a memory of the horses in the creekbed. I wrote that brief scene and liked it but found that it didn't belong in the essay. So I stored it. Writing this essay, I remembered the horses and realized the significance of the rope that tied them all together. The scene made sense in a new context. Memory seems to work that way. But what of the force that moves memory around? As the shards move roundabout and give me insight, I can't help wondering if they're waiting for me to catch up with them. Experience and preparation finally allow me to fit them into the puzzle that is my life.

Charles and I share a love of wood. We talk to each other about the craft of woodworking. He's intrigued by the angles and the geometry of construction. The wood and the grain fascinate us both. I like finishes and the processes that bring out the grain. My projects are usually small ones, and I'm as happy refinishing and restoring an old piece of furniture as I am in making a new one. I take great delight in finding beneath an old, blackened finish, a surface worthy of celebration, and I enjoy the hours spent stripping, sanding, and varnishing—working to reveal what has become hidden over time. I love the feel and the sight of the finished piece. In it I see myself and the work of those who have gone before me.

Only once did I start a new piece. It was at a time when Ann and I were at odds with each other about life. I made the rockers and the corner posts out of solid walnut, cutting the curves of the rockers across the grain, thereby accentuating the swirls and eddies in the wood. The sides came from walnut veneer plywood; they were substantial and had a beautiful simplicity after I joined them to the corner posts. I got that far and stopped, never could bring myself to join the rockers to the rest of the cradle. I imagine now that my failure had something to do with the time of life. I kept the pieces in my basement for more than ten years.

Retired now from the life of soldiering, I have my mind on other things. I write essays and try to ferret out life's secrets. I look for patterns that will give me satisfaction and stability, trying on occasion to make sense of that haunting series of questions Gauguin poses in his painting: *Where Do We Come From? What Are We? Where Are We Going?* When I stand in front of that painting in Boston's Museum of Fine Arts, my eyes home in, always, on the old crone in the lower left-hand corner. She hunkers upright in the fetal position, hands about her face, not a trace of pain. She might just have come from Munch's *The Scream* to take her place in a more serene setting, where instead of calling attention to herself in isolation, she sits down among her own, in the garden, as if nothing had ever happened, her pain gone, her place secure in the natural order. Even the question of gender is blurred by comparison. Eve, in the center of the painting, might just be Adam; the old crone the wise old man. There once again at the beginning, differences seem unimportant. Age finds context in life.

Ellisene and Charles and I have no need for cradles. Our lives have taken different turns. On my last visit to Arkansas only two or three months ago, we talked of tombstones. They had sold two plots in a fairly new cemetery and had purchased plots just made available by friends, plots in the old cemetery where Ellisene's father and our mom are buried. We went out to look over the lay of the land. While there, I took the picture of Mom's tombstone Tim had requested. He hasn't been able to go back to Hamburg since his grandmother's funeral. He figures that looking at a picture might get him ready for a visit. He's drawn back to the place but doesn't quite know how to make the trip.

About twenty years ago when I first went to a West Point reunion, I attended what seems to me now a strange memorial service. But I was moved as we walked around in the rain from grave to grave trying to find our bearing among the headstones. I remember thinking of the service later, talking about it, wondering whether any other institution in the world would inspire that kind of gathering among its graduates, especially at a reunion.

I thought not and was pleased. But I look back now wondering about us, about our youthful, male sobriety. We certainly cared about the people who were missing from our ranks, but we were lost in the graveyard. The institution had given us another maneuver, and we executed it. We went through the alien paces, step by solemn step; we got through it.

As the years passed, we shifted the sight of our gatherings, moved out of the cemetery into the beauty of the natural setting at Lusk Reservoir, close to the waters, close to the primal source of life. We gathered there at the site of the Southeast Asia memorial, out in the open, and began to sense, at least subconsciously, that we need not mourn so earnestly. We began to think less of loss and more of the lives we were pausing over. In the autumn air and the sunshine, we laughed even as we thought about the friends we missed and loved so much. Death had moved more directly into our lives, and we were learning to face it.

I learned to face it when my 120-pound Great Pyrenees died. I discovered that death left holes in the patterns of my life, and I learned too that it connected me with the living. After the dog died, Tim was disoriented each day after school; he and Snow had shared a ritual, waiting together for Ann to get home from teaching. For Tim who had lost his companion, there was emptiness to fill. The rest of us were troubled too. I kept making false starts, going down in the morning to let the dog out, planning my evening so that I could take him for the last walk of the day. I'd go downstairs sometimes out of habit, only to find emptiness. Ann felt sad that she couldn't somehow have kept him alive.

Because of Snow's death, I knew more about coping with my mom's death a few years later. I understood more fully what was going on when I picked up the phone to call and discovered halfway through the dialing that no one was at home. Loss reminded all of us of the rituals that had bound us together.

Tim's other brushes with death have made him a little skittish, and he's not yet able to think long and hard about the idea of death. As he and Patrick were growing up and we were moving back and forth across country at the Army's behest, Ann and I tried always to find our way back to Arkansas with the children. We wanted to remind them where they'd come from. Going back, we strengthened ties, found something stable in those old houses as we watched our children mingling with their kin. Over time, they watched people they loved grow old, and they learned fairly early about loss even as they were learning about love. For ten years, their grandfather fought the pain of cancer, struggled to stay alive for only one reason. He wanted to be there when the kids came home. As we drove away from his funeral, back to New York, Tim wore an old crumpled black hat that his PaPa had worn to work. Hanging now on the halltree in the foyer among my own hats, it reminds us where we've come from, where we're going.

When Ellisene and Charles told their daughter what they had done about the cemetery plots, Jo Ellen didn't much want to hear the story. She is raising a family of her own now and has just moved into a new home. Her idea, like Tim's, is to come at the graveyard indirectly, at a slant, and not too often. But I listened with interest as Ellisene told the story, and while I was home, went out to another cemetery on the outskirts of town where my father is buried. I found him in good company with his mother. They were right where they belonged.

While in Hamburg, I also went to the county library where as a young boy I used to hang out and visit Ann Veazey and Maude Pugh. They're both dead now, but many of the important county records are there, thanks to their efforts. Over the door is a memorial to Agnes Etheridge, Ann Veazey's mother—my high school English teacher. In the library, I found a new history of Ashley County, one in which Judge Etheridge's older history is reprinted. In the new part of the book, I came across this letter: "Dear Sister, I wrote to you from Gaines Landing a short time after we had completed the pleasantest part of our journey if there was any pleasure in being pent up in an old flat boat that smoked, leaked and rocked us about from pillar to post . . . from morn to night. Yet I must confess it was pleasant indeed when compared with the route through river bottom where our best travelling was four miles a day in consequence of the breaking and miring of waggons and carriages. . . . We were four weeks getting here."

The letter was written in 1848 by Elmira Marshall Hundley who had moved to Berea, Arkansas, from Clark County, Mississippi, with her husband Joel, their nine children, and one daughter-in-law. They were my maternal great-grandparents. A son, Joel Ebenezer, sixteen at the time of the move, went on to serve in the 1st Regiment, Arkansas Infantry. He returned, eventually became a cabinet maker, built houses in Berea, and married Josie Thacker who, after Joel's death, became the postmistress. She had eight living children to support. My mom was the youngest, born the year her father died.

Mom and I both grew up without our fathers. Mine left home during the war years when I was five. But his own needs claimed him, not the war. When he died years later, I stood apart at his funeral, an outsider claiming not to know him. I never felt a compelling need for him until my own sons began to call on me to be a father. Nothing in my memory served me well. As it turned out, they taught me much of what I needed to know. Without realizing it, they also taught me about loss. With them, I began to sense what I had missed without my own father. I had grown strong from his absence, but he had also cut me short without my knowing it. Yet now he seems an inseparable part of my life. Day in and day out, I see his strengths and weaknesses playing themselves out in my life, reminding me where I came from.

It may well be true that death destroys a man, but I take comfort today remembering what I read long ago: the idea of death may save him. It was the idea of death that set me off this morning when Ellisene called and unleashed a flood of memories, memories that will surely prop me up as I move toward my own end. I know that Charles, the only living father I ever had, can never leave me. Bound together as we are by life and by memory, he and I will never be free of each other. Because of him and Ellisene and our network of kin, I see more clearly the idea of life, see too how we might yet survive, all of us, the living and the dead.

Immortality

As for writing, I want to express beauty too . . . showing all the traces of the mind's passage through the world; & achieve in the end, some kind of whole made of shivering fragments; to me this seems the natural process; the flight of the mind.
VIRGINIA WOOLF

the lies of poets are lies in the service of truth
JOHN OF SALISBURY

I SIT IN MY OFFICE curtained behind the morning sun and tell myself that nothing is ever finished. For the moment, that seems to be the story of my life. And when I say those words to myself, say them over and over as I try to arrange the countless messages and all the tasks large and small that are laid out before me for the day's work, I wonder what that simple story might mean if I just relax and let my mind wander over it, making of the story what it will.

Nothing is ever finished. Nothing.

When Joan Didion reminds us that we tell ourselves stories in order to live, she has in mind a saving act of desperation. For her, storytelling arrests the "shifting phantasmagoria" of life, puts a stop to the movement. Didion is on to something, of course, but I think she's a little shy of the truth. We tell ourselves stories not so much to order the chaotic but to reach an understanding, perhaps indirectly, of the lives we are living. Our stories do freeze the frames of our experience, but those stories also carry meaning as old as life itself. Embedded in each is a nugget of truth. The truth varies, of course, according to the way we tell the stories. But without them, we are lost, alone, cut adrift. Stories provide context and continuity. Without them we begin to think there's nothing left to say, nothing left to write. With them we keep our lives at the center of our imaginations—just where they belong.

MY MOTHER spent much of her life—about forty of her ninety years—running a bus station in a small south Arkansas town. She went to the station day in and day out during all those years, meeting the buses, serving the customers, entertaining friends and their children, providing a home away from home in the most unlikely place—"A place," she'd say, "where folks could sit down and take the load off their feet." She's been dead six years, and I still can't get her out of my head. Her life sits at the center of my imagination, a monument against the ravages of time. She's not at all a lifeless thing.

Today, her words about endurance come back again. "Honey," she'd say, "what can't be cured must be endured." The simplest of stories. A cliché, perhaps, out of any mouth but hers. She lost two husbands, one to cancer, the other to a wandering spirit, a son to war. She lived alone almost twenty-five years, finally gave up the bus station at eighty-five, in the aftermath of a tornado that left her hunkered under an old oak desk, rain pouring through the roof destroying her most prized possessions—the pictures and letters and cards from family and friends. But even in the nursing home, later, she managed somehow to gather about her the fragments, the bits and pieces from here and there that pleased her—a favorite chair from my brother, pictures, lots of pictures, on the tables, in the drawers, on the walls, cards from grandchildren, a telephone right by her head, and always a small box of stationery on the bedside table. She wrote as best she could against the palsied movement of her hand, telling her stories until almost the day she died, writing out the wisdom of her life. Even at the very end, her mind was razor sharp, memory serving her, steadying her spirit. She had a hold on things. The stories she had in her head did it for her, I suspect. Simple stories.

What can't be cured must be endured.

My father, I had thought in my younger days, couldn't be endured. He left us high and dry when I was five, and I had reason over time to resent him. There were embarrassing moments through my school days when he wouldn't come back for the big events, and there were other times when he would come bleary-eyed and a bit tipsy, glowing with false pride. I felt distanced from him then, out of touch, almost as if I didn't know him. But finally, his not being there made little difference. He hadn't been around for the daily rituals, hadn't had time for commitment. He had consumed his life living it, and nothing from the living spilled over for the rest of us.

Over the years, trying to face my own self, I have come to love and respect my father's wandering spirit. I know now how compelling the heart can be, and I imagine he had no choice but to follow his wherever it took him. But the loving spirit that led him on and gave him satisfaction also did him in. He lived a less cerebral life than I do, a life closer to the bone. He knew little, if anything, about restraint. I'm a luckier man. I sit and write and sustain myself with stories, chasing always my dad and the others I have loved. He had no knack for storytelling; never knew much about the mana of the mind. I have no idea what he thought, ever . . . and know only a little, even today, about what he did. I suspect though that memory served him ill, that he never knew the storyteller's peace, that he simply couldn't reconcile his heart to the daily grind, couldn't fit the pieces of his life together and settle his restlessness.

In the thick of middle age, I long to sit uninterrupted for lazy stretches of time or to lollygag outdoors, meandering away from people and organizations and schedules. I have to contend with a touch of my father's restlessness, but I'm more interested in solitude now than adventure. I yearn to do my wandering over a patch of ground that might bless me occasionally with surprise. I have a younger friend who has moved to the country with acres and acres of land, and she has begun to move over that bounded space, exploring its contours, observing its wildlife, learning the promise and the confinement afforded by fences and good neighbors. Today she called to tell me that she and her husband may have to give it up. The farm is one of twenty-five targeted sites for the dumping of toxic wastes. A lawyer by profession, she understands the processes that can claim her space; she knows about the laws of dominion. But the slightest prospect of personal, legal entanglements rustles her spirit, and her mind moves quickly to devise schemes of surrender that will keep her life free of legal brambles, even if it means giving up the land without a fight. She doesn't want to have to walk around the law when she roams over the fields.

Solitude is hard to come by these days, and I, like my friend, yearn for it. I need more time for the stories. Behind the urge to put all the pieces of my life together there seems to be a gathering instinct at work, something driving me back into memory and out into the world, something compelling me to bring the pieces together. It's as if I'm finally beginning to understand that going down far enough into my own soul is the same as going out into the world. I can do both simultaneously, and when I do, I begin to unearth nuggets of truth. Finding those surprises seems to be my primary business as I search for a clearer picture, hoping to find there in the images of my life the earth's treasure.

This searching may very well be a matriarchal thing. It's certainly not the kind of searching my dad did. Nor is it the kind of searching I did as a young Army officer. Eleven or so years after graduating from West Point, after my first stint with troops in Virginia and Korea, after a year and a half of graduate school at the University of Pennsylvania, after three years of teaching writing and literature at West Point, after all that, I chose these representative words for the plaque the English department gave me as I left West Point to rejoin the Regular Army: "The ULTIMATE most holy form of theory is action. . . . It is not God who will save us—it is we who will save God, by battling, by creating, and by transmuting matter into spirit." I look at those words now and think of the naive and necessary heroism that lay behind my efforts. I had loved the brashness and the struggle to excel, knowing that I had to act, had to learn to stand on my own. But there came a time when action seemed less important than contemplation. When I discovered that the Army was claiming my heart and my mind and that I was losing my place beside my children, I had to face a hard and necessary fact: I would not be able to stay on that imaginary train that could take me one day to the Chief of Staff's office in Washington. I wasn't cut out for it.

What I was cut out for was teaching. During those early years in the Army, whether leading troops or working with cadets at West Point, I had been a teacher. My greatest satisfaction had not come from commanding but from developing young men who were learning to live together in a community, many for the first time. Everywhere I went, I was teaching, teaching how to prepare the Nike Hercules missile for firing, how to fire and maintain a howitzer, how to compute the firing data that would put artillery rounds on the target, how to assemble nuclear weapons, how to select and occupy field positions in a combat zone, how to keep men alive and effective in the middle of a rice paddy in Vietnam, how to coordinate and manage the activities of a battalion of artillery. Every one of those tasks required teamwork and cooperation and intensive training, and in each of those places where I worked, I was the trainer, the teacher. When the time came for graduate school and an assignment back to the West Point faculty, I chose to study literature rather than mathematics or thermodynamics, subjects the career counselor in Washington urged me to consider because they had more utility. My imagination led me to the stories. I was interested in literature as a way into life.

What I found at the University of Pennsylvania surprised me. I was not prepared for the literary historians on Penn's faculty, some of whom, even in the late sixties, were just getting to the New Critics. Only two of my teachers put the primary texts, the stories themselves, at the center of their classes. Both encouraged us to set the critics aside and read with lively imaginations. They encouraged us to reach out and connect, to imagine that there were new answers to life's old problems. They seemed to know that the stories we were reading stretched back in time and forward, and that if we read them with care and diligence, they might reveal a pearl of great value.

It was in Herbert Howarth's class that I first read *The Man Who Died*, that little novella D. H. Lawrence wrote at the end of his life on earth. Lawrence's consuming rage for understanding still fascinates me. He wanted to possess the knowledge of what it meant to be man and woman living together—in bed and in culture. Marriage was always out there in front of him, tormenting, leading, beckoning him toward understanding, and he never tired of the search that compelled him to fit the pieces together. In *The Man Who Died*, he tells us about the life of Christ following the resurrection, insisting that the resurrection story has no meaning unless Christ comes back flesh and blood, back into life a man, freed of his own consuming urge to save God by battling, by creating, by transmuting flesh into spirit. Lawrence insists on bringing Christ back resurrected, erect and upright, a living man.

The resurrection itself required a woman; it always does. Coming back from the dead is serious business, too serious, I suspect, to leave to the men . . . even in Lawrence's imagination. As the foundation for his story, Lawrence turned to the Egyptian myth of Isis and Osiris. There he found the image of a woman who could take the broken body of Christ and resurrect it; she could bring him back to life. Isis twice had her husband taken away, each time by a jealous brother, Seth. When Isis found Osiris's body the first time and returned it to Egypt, Seth cut it into fourteen pieces and scattered them throughout Egypt. Again Isis lovingly and dutifully went after Osiris, this time seeking to gather all the pieces and reassemble her husband's body. She found all of him except the genitals and therefore had to make an image of the phallus, fashioning it out of wax and spices. Having put the severed parts of Osiris's body together again, she resuscitated him long enough to conceive Horus who would revenge their suffering.

What interests me, and what interested Lawrence, about this story is not Osiris's heroic kingship but Isis's loving devotion, her configuring imagination, and her defiance in the face of established order. In the end, she had the gods granting her favors. Like Lawrence, I am intrigued by her persistence, by her relentless effort to search for and find, to collect and reassemble, the lost or scattered parts of her husband's body. Were I to be blessed by a goddess in my life, I would wish her to be Isis. In her search, I find the story of my life, the meaning at the very heart of things. I find there the key to my life as teacher and writer.

Writing has always been for me an act of collecting and reconfiguring, imagining and reconceiving, a reaching out into life and libraries to find meaning. I have, like searching Isis, been trying to find the pieces that would make life whole—a task that's never finished. The search itself carries over to my classroom, where day after day and year after year I try to set in motion searches like that of the mythic woman who's always hovering in the back of my mind. I want my students to be grasped by a single necessity that will set their minds in motion and engender the gathering instinct. I want them to know that the search has no value unless they aim to unearth the mythic nuggets, the stories and the ideas that give us bearing, connecting us with our past and leading us into the future.

Each year as a prelude to more formal, academic writing, I try to put students in an exploratory frame of mind, setting them free to follow what my friend Sam Pickering calls the "vagaries of their own willful curiosities." I send them back into memory, asking only that they retrieve a fragment from their past. What I want them to find, of course, is not some lifeless thing, but a story stolen out of time, a story that reverberates and plays on their imaginations. I want the students to be able to pluck that initial fragment out of memory so that they can set it beside other fragments and begin to make sense of things . . . if only temporarily.

It's not just a simple matter of telling a story. The stories constitute the foundation, but their inherent truths are not always self-evident. Only the writer can bring them together, arranging and shaping them to reveal the missing part, the *idea* itself. That idea must be configured, must be imagined. The stories generate it, but the writer, having gathered the stories together, must decide, finally, what they mean. Meaning, however elusive and changing, is the hidden nugget, that treasure the imagination seeks. Behind that never-ending search is the urge to understand, the human need to make things whole, to create something lasting.

About a year ago, when I was writing an essay about soldiering, I asked my students how young men and women at Harvard might be heroic, suggesting to them at the outset that my own notions about heroism had changed over time, that acts of physical grandeur now seem far less important to me than acts of mind. I wanted them to think a little bit about the never-ending struggle for self-definition. I was hoping too that I would be able to get them to think about how some of our heroic urges carry over into the latter stages of life, depriving us of solace. I wanted them to think about what a hero is supposed to do when the spaces on the map have been charted, when there is no longer a home to protect, a family to nurture, a beast to slay, a war to win. How do men and women sustain themselves when the tasks have been completed or when there is no cultural need for the old heroics? I gave the briefest sketch of what I had in mind, and discovered very quickly that my own middle-aged dis-ease didn't interest them.

My students had notions of heroism that differed markedly from mine, differed even from those I had when I was their age. Many spoke of their struggle to develop a voice that could meet the voice behind the lectern in their classroom. They spoke of the enormous difficulty of facing day after day the respected voices of authority all over the university. They talked too of the importance of thinking hard enough, struggling actually, to utter a response, to say something finally that would make them feel satisfied with themselves. One young woman, having listened long enough to the men in the room, spoke of the difficulty at Harvard of being smart and being pretty. She said that in the minds of the men, it was impossible to be both. You couldn't be both and be a Harvard woman. To try was to be heroic. A pall fell over the room as she adjusted herself in the chair, tucked her legs up into the seat beneath her skirt, and faced them.

Following close order on the heels of that discussion, Elizabeth began a new essay. Intrigued by Ingres's *La Grande Odalisque,* she saw in the painting a woman whose "fluid" body is "anatomically impossible: the back and arm are far too long and her legs cross over each other in what would be a highly uncomfortable position for anyone with solid bones." She saw this woman as an "enigma," just as she saw something "fraudulent" about Rita Hayworth's *Gilda* who "was a whore and a virtuous woman . . . two women inhabiting a beautiful shell whose two sides were irreconcilable." Elizabeth thought of these two women in terms of an ideal woman of her own, one she occasionally drew in the margins of her notebook. She brought all these women together in her essay, placing them alongside scenes from her life that accentuated her own struggle to control her weight, to make her body thin by following a "regimen" that alternated days of eating "enormous amounts" with days of fasting.

In junior high school, Elizabeth turned to "self-induced vomiting" to maintain her own façade. In my class, she turned to Yeats to clarify her idea about beauty:

> There is a line in Yeats' "Adam's Curse" that cries bitterness—
>
> > To be born woman is to know—
> > Although they do not talk of it at school—
> > That we must labor to be beautiful
>
> I have only just discovered that I have been misquoting these lines for years. In my mind the last line, though essentially the same, has always had a slightly different nuance. . . . We must suffer to be beautiful.

Therein lies the story of Elizabeth's heroism: We must suffer to be beautiful. Turning to Yeats, she turns away from the autobiographical details of her life to the idea itself. Her story gives us insight, reminds us about the perils of beauty, and asks us indirectly to think about how we create those perils. The essay itself is deeply rooted in the particularity of Elizabeth's own experiences—her stories as well as her treasures from the art museum—but she tells her tale in such a way that it links us all together. Leaving her essay, we know that Elizabeth will have to endure forever in a culture where beauty inflicts intense pain. The rest of us, because of her tale, will probably never see beauty again in the same light.

Virginia Woolf once reminded us that emotion is also form. She had in mind something other than the architectonic scaffolding Percy Lubbock thought of as structure. Woolf saw through that surface order to something much deeper, something emotional, something deeply felt, that sets in motion the play of our mind on paper. That movement of mind, that grounded search, leads to the mythic nuggets—the larger, more comprehensive treasure we fashion out of the waxy substance of our imaginations, those ideas that give meaning to our struggles.

AT THE VERY BEGINNING of *The Unbearable Lightness of Being*, Milan Kundera expresses concern that each generation seems destined to relive the same old stories. He wonders quite simply what the myth of the eternal return might "signify." According to Kundera's reckoning, "We must live our lives without knowing in advance the answer to life's most troubling questions. And what can life be worth," he asks, "if the first rehearsal for life is life itself?" Yet in the end, Kundera seems to take comfort in the happiness his characters find against the sad fact of recurrence. The lives that Thomas, Sabina, and Tereza live are no more perfect than the lives any of us live, and yet, in Kundera's mind, there is happiness.

"The sadness was the form," he says, "the happiness content."

Kundera, like Didion, I think, is a little shy of the truth. We do indeed tell ourselves stories in order to live; the stories themselves order our lives and record our occasional happiness. So be it. But we also tell ourselves stories to satisfy a restless and insatiable urge to understand why we are living. Stories give us bearing, stabilize us . . . momentarily. They also record our legacy; they are the human trace we spread across the world, recording our movement from generation to generation. If we lay those generational stories side by side, we find the history of our progress and our failure.

Kundera's modern mind, looking at the story of the eternal return asks, in a thoroughly modern way, what the myth can *signify* . . . as if he's afraid of the old-fashioned word meaning, as if he can't risk an intellectual foray into *meaning* itself. Yet there's something old-fashioned and traditional in his question, no matter how he chooses to frame it. Kundera is not, after all, "nothing but a devouring flame of thought" like Matthew Arnold's Empedocles, who was compelled in the face of the modern dilemma to *take* his life as a retreat from "despondency and gloom." For Kundera, there is at least the content that is happiness.

But there is more. There is possibility and promise in those stories we tell ourselves. If the stories never change, if we are destined to repeat them over and over, generation after generation, it is because we fail to read them as if our very lives depend on them. If we see in them a pattern that compels us to live as our forebears have always lived, they bequeath a burden that is unbearably heavy. But if, occasionally, we can look beneath the surface into the form that is emotion, we might just catch a glimpse of the very impulses that set our lives in motion. We may discover that there are indeed new possibilities, new ways to live out the impulses. We may find that the old heroics no longer seem worthy of our imaginations . . . or our lives.

As I continue to gather the fragments of my own life, I like to think that the stories I tell myself have something to do with other lives, that my story could be everyone's. I know of course that the larger story I'm trying to tell will not be finished. Nothing ever is. As I give in to my own needs, wandering and looking for solitude so that I can find time to let my gathering instinct reveal new secrets to me, as I sit and wait and try to open myself to the wisdom of the stories themselves, I am sustained by a rhythm of involvement that binds me to those I love and chase in my imagination, whether they be the living or the dead. And like my mom, I continue to write. The smaller stories steady me against the ravages of time; they teach me about endurance and quell my wandering spirit, reminding me to sit still, telling me that this is the only life I'll ever live. From them, on the best of occasions, I relax into life's complexities, and I garner, if only for a moment, the storyteller's peace, the revelation that even the fragments of my own life can shiver into wholeness.

www.ingramcontent.com/pod-product-compliance
Lightning Source LLC
Chambersburg PA
CBHW011950150426
43195CB00018B/2886